Abo'

Tony was born in Nottingham, Eng   twenties the seeds were sown for his love affair with Gr   aring a holiday on the island of Skiathos. Since then he has vis   d many of the islands of the Ionian and Aegean seas, as well as the mainland of Greece.

His heart though lies on the small, unspoilt islands of the Aegean. When in 2006, he had the opportunity of retiring from his business consultancy, he and his partner Carol chose Thassos as their base as UK ex-pats, selecting to live on the outskirts of Thassos Town, known locally as Limenas.

As an author of business books, Tony had been aware after his many years travelling within Greece that what was lacking for the holidaymaker and general traveller was a comprehensive, honest and accurate guide to each island in an easy to read book.

In 2006 he wrote his first travel guide on his adopted island home of Thassos. The reviews received were excellent and the book achieved high sales both in Europe and the United States.

And so, in 2007, he wrote his second book on Kos followed by this book on the island of Santorini in 2008. His latest travel guide covers the island of Rhodes and was first published in January 2013. Tony hopes that in the years to come, his continuing travels will allow him to write guides for more of the Greek islands that he loves.

Opposite: The Boxing Youths fresco from the ancient archaeological site of Akrotiri, circa 17th century B.C. (*Museum of Prehistoric Thira*)

A-Z Guide to

Santorini

Tony Oswin

Contents:
The island, its history, what to see, where to go, eating out,
entertainment, the best beaches, travel information and a host
of tips and hints for the holidaymaker and traveller.

2018 Edition

Published January 2018 by arima publishing

www.arimapublishing.com

ISBN: 978-1-84549-718-7

11th edition

Printed and bound in the United Kingdom

Typeset in Arial

This book is sold subject to the conditions that it shall not, by way of trade or otherwise, be lent, re-sold, hired out, or otherwise circulated without the publisher's prior consent in any form of binding or cover other than that which it is published and without a similar condition including this condition being imposed on the subsequent purchaser.

DISCLAIMER
The contents of these materials are for general guidance only and are not intended to apply in specific circumstances. As such, the contents of these materials should not be relied on for the purpose of deciding to do, or omitting to do anything, and you should always seek independent advice in relation to any particular question or requirement you might have. Any opinions set out in these materials are those of the author only, and unless expressly stated otherwise, are not the opinions of the publisher. To the fullest extent permitted by law, the publisher and Tony Oswin expressly disclaims any and all liability and responsibility to any person, in respect of the consequences of anything done, or omitted to be done, in reliance on the contents of these materials.

Arima Publishing, ASK House, Northgate Avenue
Bury St. Edmunds, Suffolk, IP32 6BB
T: (+44) 01284 700321

www.arimapublishing.com

To Carol for all her loving support

Foreword

I have been visiting Greece for over thirty years and during that time I have fallen in love with the country, its people and most of all the Greek approach to life.

However, during my travels I always found it difficult to obtain island specific guide books, written in English and containing up to the minute information and advice. Too many times, I returned home from a visit to Greece, only to talk to someone who advised me of something to do or see that I had been unaware of.

After moving to Greece in 2006, I realised that I now had the time and opportunity to fulfil that need, starting with a guide book on my adopted home island of Thassos. This, the third book in the series, is aimed at helping you to get the most out of your time on the dramatic island of Santorini. I hope that you will find it helpful and informative, both in planning your holiday and during your stay.

Due to the wonders of modern publishing, the information in the book is updated on a regular basis and I would appreciate your feedback by email to help keep the book focused on readers needs. Through this and my regular research visits to the island, I aim to keep the book fresh, comprehensive and accurate.

Occasionally I have been asked why there are no photographs in the book? When I first set out to write my travel guides, one major objective was to make sure the books were accurate and with the latest information at an affordable price. To achieve this, the publication process I chose was POD (*Print on Demand*), whereby each book is printed at the time of order, from a manuscript that is regularly updated. However, one drawback of POD is that at present, the addition of colour photographs adds considerably to the cost of each book.

As is the practice with books containing photographs, if they are to be offered at a reasonable price, they are printed in bulk to reduce the unit cost. This inevitably means that at these quantities, the book can be significantly out of date when purchased.

I hope you therefore agree that my decision to move all the media to the supporting website, so as to offer you both the highest quality and ensure the accuracy of information in the book, was the correct one.

As both official and local organisations have a habit of not releasing tourist related news, or information on tourist events until a few days before they start, I strongly recommend that you visit the website regularly whilst on the island. The latest news from the island is updated throughout each day to keep you constantly informed.

I wish you a wonderful 2018 holiday,

Tony Oswin

Our website can be found at:-

www.atoz-guides.com

(*your password can be found on the 'Acknowledgements' page at the back of this book*)

Our email address is:-

info@atoz-guides.com

A to Z Travel Club

Unique amongst travel guides, the 'A to Z' guides are designed in two parts. The printed book, which contains all the information you need on your travels around the island and the 'A to Z' website, which offers a wealth of supporting information. The website also allows us to bring you the very latest tourist news from the island, special 'members' offers and more high quality photographs and videos than with any other travel guide, including over 50 photographs, panoramas, videos and webcams on the island.

All this is totally free to you and is accessed via a member's password. You will find your member password at the bottom of the 'Acknowledgements' page at the back of this book.

To access the full member benefits of the website, place your cursor over the 'Travel Club' button at the top of any website page. Next move your cursor down over 'Travel Club Santorini' and a further drop down menu appears, then place your cursor over the desired page and click:-

Santorini News - Tourist news updated throughout each day

Holiday Advice - A wide range of holiday related advice

Discounts & Offers - Holiday ideas and money saving offers

2D Gallery - Over 50 high quality photographs, and videos

Santorini Weather - Real-time weather and an 8 day forecast

Santorini Travel Info - Flight information, money matters etc.

Santorini Maps & Panoramas - Print-off maps and panoramas

Santorini Links - Webcams and a range of Santorini websites

www.atoz-guides.com

Contents

Santorini

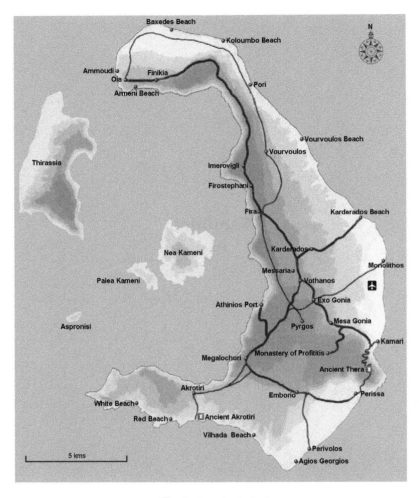

□ Archaeological sites

Due to the small size of the book, we are unable to include a more detailed map. However, if you visit our website there are basic and detailed maps of the island to download and print off. Alternatively there are free maps available from most car hire companies and many other businesses once you arrive on the island.

The spectacular island of Santorini

Santorini (*Greek - Σαντορίνη*) is a small circular shaped archipelago of islands of volcanic origin, located in the southern Aegean Sea 110 kilometres north of the island of Crete and is the most southern of the Cyclades group of islands. In antiquity it was known as both Strongoli (*the circular one*) and Kallistē (*the beautiful one*), with the name of Santorini originating in the 13th century A.D., a derivative of Saint Irene. Herodotus (*c.484 - c.425 B.C.*), quotes the name of the island as being Thira in his book "The Histories" and that is the official name it is known as today.

The islands making up the archipelago have an area of 73 sq km and a population of approximately 13,000. Consisting of the main horse-shoe shaped island of Santorini, to the northwest the smaller island of Thirasia and within the lagoon the two volcanic cones of Palea and Nea Kameni, the latter two being uninhabited. Neither of the main islands have rivers, which means that water is scarce. Until the late 20th century the population had to collect rain water in cisterns, supplementing this with spring-water and supplies imported from overseas. Today there is a modern desalination plant that provides clean water to most areas.

The main island of Santorini is one of the most scenic islands of the Aegean. Whether during the day, when you can marvel at the moon-like landscapes, or by night, when both sunsets and moonsets can be viewed from exactly the same spot, you can't help but be enthralled.

Once a major exporter of pumice, the quarries were closed in 1986 to protect the volcanic caldera and now the primary industry is tourism, which in summer, significantly increases the resident population. Santorini's spectacular natural beauty and many attractions make it one of Greece's top tourist destinations.

Santorini can boast a small but successful wine industry, based on the grape variety Assyrtiko, which is resistant to Phylloxera (*an insect related to the common aphid*) that ravaged other European wine producing countries in the early 20th century. Assyrtiko vines are well adapted to the volcanic soils of Santorini, pruned to form low spiralling baskets of foliage, these baskets protect the grapes growing inside from any chilling winds. The vines are widely planted, as their main source of water is nocturnal dew and sea mist. The white wines of Santorini are very dry, with a strong citrus scent and a slight sulphurous flavour, a result of the islands volcanic soils.

A traditional wine produced on the island is Vinsanto, which is a honey coloured white, sweet and an extremely strong dessert wine. The wine is made from sun-dried grapes and barrel-aged, which are both responsible for its colour and strength.

Santorini has its own international airport and is also a regular stop-off point for the many cruise liners that ply the Aegean.

The main settlements on Santorini are Fira, Oia (*pronounced Eea*), Emborio, Kamari, Imerovigli, Pyrgos and Thirassia.

Fira, the island's capital, has approximately 3,000 permanent residents and is dramatically perched high on the cliffs overlooking the central lagoon. Your first glimpse of Fira, from your plane or ship, will be the myriad of whitewashed houses that resemble a scatter of sugar cubes on the cliff top.

The formation of the lagoon

Santorini was once a complete island with a typical central volcanic peak. However, during the final throws of a major eruption 120,000 years ago, the subterranean roof of the emptied magma chamber collapsed, taking with it both the flanks of the volcano and most of the island. This created a breach to the sea, which resulted in the flooding of the massively enlarged caldera, forming one of the largest on earth and creating the basic topography we see today.

During the following millennia, eruptions of the undersea volcanic vent finally created an island within the caldera (*similar to today's Nea Kameni*). This evidently lay dormant for a long period of time up to the late Bronze Age, as testified to by the frescoes found at Akrotiri that clearly show the central island inhabited. It was then that this central volcano catastrophically erupted and followed the same cycle of collapsing in on itself and disappearing under the lagoon.

Recent Dendrochronological research*, ice-core findings in Greenland and radiocarbon dating of organic remains, indicate that this eruption occurred in 1627 B.C (*+/-one year*). However, this date conflicts with that previously determined from archaeological evidence, which places the event between 1550 and 1500 B.C. My personal opinion is that the ice-core and Dendrochronological date is accurate, but as the precise chronology is still in dispute, I shall henceforth just refer to the event as the "Minoan eruption".

The lagoon now measures 11km by 7km and is surrounded by cliffs that rise to 300 metres on three sides. The cliffs plunge spectacularly down to the lagoon, which at its deepest is almost 400 metres. On the fourth side of the island, the lagoon is separated from the Aegean by a much smaller island called Thirassia. This island is all that remains of the western flanks of the original volcano. The seaward flanks of the island on the north, east and southern sides slope down to the coastal agricultural areas.

All the island's ports are sited within the lagoon, as it has been seen to provide safe harbour for even the largest liners. A record sadly broken in 2007 (*see page 50*).

The Minoan eruption

There is evidence of at least twelve major explosive eruptions in the last 200,000 years on Santorini. The Minoan eruption was though, one of the world's largest volcanic events in the last 10,000 years, estimated to have been ten times the magnitude of the Krakatoa eruption. About 60 cubic km (*14 cubic miles*) of magma and ash was ejected.

During the initial phase of the eruption, the Plinian column (*named after 'Pliny the Younger', a famous Roman writer who described the Vesuvius eruption of 79 A.D.*) rose to over 48km (*30 miles*) into the stratosphere. The removal of such a large volume of magma eventually caused the volcano, centred in the middle of the ancient flooded caldera, to collapse in on itself and disappear under the lagoon. Ash fell over a large area of the eastern and southern Mediterranean and the collapse and subsequent explosion resulted in a catastrophic tsunami, estimated to have reached 40 metres in height. The ash and gases released caused major metrological and environmental damage throughout the eastern Mediterranean and in fact across the whole northern hemisphere. No trace of the islanders themselves has yet been found, but the present theory is that the pressures that this event placed on the Minoan civilisation as a whole, laid the seeds for its final collapse. It is interesting that around the time of the eruption, there was a fundamental change in Minoan art on Crete, from the glorification of athletics and the human form to what seems to be a fixation with all aspects of the sea and marine life. Was this a result of the psychological impact of both the eruption and the subsequent tsunami on the Minoans?

The many historical eruptions mean that the Santorini of today exhibits a complex stratification of overlapping shield volcano layering. Basalt and andesite lava flows that make up the shields can be seen as banded layers in the cliff below the town of Fira. Whilst some of the cliff is thought to be a caldera wall associated with an eruption 21,000 year ago, the white layer at the top is the tephra (*air-borne ash*) from the Minoan eruption.

After the Minoan eruption, there was a period of 1400 years, during which the volcano once again remained dormant. Then in 198 B.C. the volcano came alive, with an eruption centred in the middle of the lagoon emanating from volcanic vents below the sea; this created a new island called Hierra. In 46 A.D. a further eruption created another island, Theia. Finally, in 60 A.D. a third eruption united these two islands in to what is now called Palea Kameni (*palea = old and Kameni = burnt*). For the next 700 years the volcano lay dormant, then in 726, it once again erupted, increasing the size of Palea Kameni, with two further eruptions in 1457 and 1508 adding further material. The present height of the island is 110 metres above sea level.

In 1650 eruptions in a new area of the lagoon created a further islet, then called Mikra Kameni (*mikra = small*). In 1707, further activity near Mikra created two new volcanic domes. They were called Aspronisi and Macronesi. Those were united in the course of the following five years by an island which formed between Palea and Mikra Kameni, much larger and higher than either and was called Nea Kameni (*nea = new*). This new island holds the distinction of being the youngest in Greece.

The major volcanic eruptions since the Minoan eruption date to 197 B.C., 1866, 1925 and 1949-1950. The latter eruption on Nea Kameni was phreatic (*explosive eruptions due to the hot magma coming in contact with water*) and lasted less than a month. This eruption constructed a dome and produced lava flows. In 1956 Santorini suffered a major earthquake, although not followed by any volcanic activity it caused severe damage on the island and resulted in the death of 49 people. Other volcanic vents on the archipelago include Akritiri, Thira, Skaros, Megalo Vouno, Mikro Profitis Ilias and Thirassia.

Santorini is renowned for the beautiful views from the villages situated on the cliffs of the lagoon and archipelago. These are especially magnificent at sunset. Tourists can visit the volcanic islands of Paleo and Nea Kameni by taking one of the daily cruises. Once on the shore of the larger island Nea Kameni, you can walk through the moon-like scenery and visit the volcano's crater and sulphuric steam vents.

Atlantis

No history of Santorini would be complete without a reference to Santorini being linked with the fabled Atlantis.

Whilst the debate continues, it is a fact that academics have a reputation for being habitual sceptics. Only when a so-called outlandish theory is proved correct, does everyone seem to jump on the bandwagon. It is then hard to find anyone who will admit that they initially ridiculed the theory in question! I personally place more weight on the accuracy of both written and oral tradition and believe that the stories of Atlantis are like many others, based on the distant memory of a real event.

The story of Atlantis originated in Egypt and was first reported in the 7th century B.C. Many centuries later Plato, the famous Greek philosopher and writer, heard the story and was so captivated that he recorded it for posterity. Plato's account describes Atlantis in detail and during early excavations at the archaeological site of Akrotiri, a fresco was found in the ruins depicting the island of Santorini as it was prior to the catastrophic Minoan eruption. What is striking is how close the scenes depicted on the fresco match the description of Atlantis. Plato also writes that Atlantis had quarries where "rocks of white, black, and red were extracted from the hills and used to construct a great island city". This description matches the unique composition of the geology found on Santorini.

Some sceptics have argued that Santorini could not be a candidate for the location of Atlantis as Plato describes it as "an island which was larger than Libya and Asia together". However, what they do not take into account is that the island was only one of many Minoan colonies in the Mediterranean and Aegean regions which included Crete, the largest of the Greek islands. It is entirely plausible that the original Egyptian narrative referred to all the Minoan territories that were destroyed, not just Santorini. Most if not all of these colonies would have been sited on or near shorelines and as we saw through the tragic events on Boxing Day 2004 in the Indian Ocean and more recently in Japan in 2011, Mega-Tsunamis have the power to sweep away whole communities across a vast area. The recent discovery of seashells dated to the late 1600's B.C. deposited high above the seashore on Crete, linked with the archaeological evidence confirming that at this time the Minoan civilisation as a whole went into a steep decline and we have all the hallmarks of a catastrophic disaster centred on Santorini.

What we do know is that Egypt was an important trading partner of the Minoans on Crete, who were known to them as the Keftiu. However, no records have yet been found to confirm whether the Egyptians also regarded the inhabitants of Santorini as Keftiu, if they traded with them and what was their name for the island.

As Linear A (*the Minoan script*) has yet to be deciphered, we do not know if there are any Minoan written records of the eruption, but other eastern Mediterranean civilisations aside from the Egyptians, noted catastrophic events at this time. Dendrochronology* results from tree samples as far away as Ireland and California record adverse weather effects on tree growth and even more amazing, the Chinese recorded unusual climatic changes in the same period.

My own view is that I find it implausible that such a devastating event as the Minoan eruption would go totally unrecorded and that the evidence so far points strongly to the likelihood that Santorini was in fact, in the eyes of the Egyptians, the location of Atlantis. Inevitably one has to say that until irrefutable evidence is found, the sceptics will continue to be unconvinced. I will leave it to the reader to judge the evidence so far available and decide which events are likely to have led to the creation of the Atlantis story.

Exodus

Recently, the Minoan eruption has also been linked by some scientists and theologians, to events portrayed in the biblical account of the exodus of the Hebrews out of Egypt. Certainly many of the "Ten Plagues of Egypt" have been recorded as occurring during and after other major volcanic eruptions. A further theory links the account of the parting of the Red Sea** to the effects of a tsunami. As we all saw through the images from the 2004 Boxing Day and Japanese tsunamis, the sea initially rushes out from the coast, just prior to the tidal wave arriving.

This new evidence linked with the Minoan eruption has allowed some to postulate that prior to a resulting tsunami striking Egypt, there was a withdrawal of seawater from the coastal reed marshes. This could have made such areas temporarily passable to the Hebrews. However, the subsequent tidal wave would result in the devastation of anyone, or anything in the area. This would clearly make the story of the Exodus more plausible.

Any proof of the hypothesis is yet to be found and therefore the best that can be said is that it is an interesting theory.

* Dendrochronology or tree-ring dating is the method of scientific dating, based on the analysis of tree-ring growth patterns. Changes in climatic conditions directly affect a trees growth pattern and therefore the size of its annual growth rings. These changes can be linked to such events as major volcanic eruptions and can be dated by cross-referencing a particular growth pattern to a library of tree rings of known date.

** Recent research has confirmed that the reference to the Red Sea in the story of the Exodus is actually inaccurate, having resulted from a mistranslation from the original Hebrew texts. The correct translation refers to the "Sea of Reeds".

The future for Santorini

Taking into account the volcanic history of Santorini and that the latest island that has formed, Nea Kameni, is once again of the Cinder Dome category of volcano *(made up of loose volcanic rock and ash)*, it is highly likely that sometime in the future there will be another catastrophic Minoan style eruption.

The likelihood is that during such an eruption, the magma chamber will empty putting great strain on the roof of the chamber. With the overlying volcano being inherently unstable, the roof will fail and the volcano will collapse in on itself, once again generating a Mega-Tsunami in the Mediterranean region.

History

Prehistoric to classical period

According to the evidence found in Santorini's main archaeological sites, the first human presence on the island dates back to at least the Neolithic Period. Traces of settlement on the island found at Akrotiri date to around 3600 B.C. and confirm that the island was inhabited from the pre-Bronze Age.

Certainly the island was inhabited by either the Minoans, or a people with a very similar culture, as discoveries made at Akrotiri and Red Beach confirm. The evidence shows without doubt, that they were a highly sophisticated and cultured people. Their art is stylistically the same as that found on the island of Crete, such as Knossos, with many wall paintings and pottery showing naturalistic portrayals of animals and people in the same ancient Minoan style. The catastrophic Minoan eruption though seems to have brought to an end any habitation on the island, with no indication having been found of occupation during the following three centuries.

Evidence shows that around 1300 B.C., the Phoenicians settled on ancient Thira and stayed until about 1200 B.C. Then, around 1100 B.C., the island came under the control of the Lacedaemonians of mainland Greece, better known as the Spartans.

In the 9th century B.C., Dorians from north-western Greece (*one of the four ancient Greek tribes*) founded the main Hellenic city (*Ancient Thera*) on the peak of Mesa Vouno, 396 metres above sea level. It is said that the city was named after their leader Theras.

A number of Dorian stone inscriptions have been found in the ruins of the city, especially in the vicinity of the Temple of Apollo, describing pederastic relationships in the community. Pederasty is a relationship between an adolescent boy and an adult male, who is not a direct family member. The intended aim at that time was that the adult (*known as the erastes*) would mentor and educate their eromenoi (*the ancient Greek name for a boy*) until manhood. However, many ancient scripts attest to these relationships also being sexual in nature.

In ancient Sparta, young boys left their mother at the age of seven to join the agoge, the all-male institution, where the adolescents lived and underwent military training and moral teaching until the age of twenty.

In the 7th and 6th centuries B.C., Thira had commercial and trade relations with most of the islands and cities of Greece and founded cities elsewhere in the Mediterranean, such a Cyrene on the coast of Libya.

In the 5th century B.C., Dorian Thira refused to join the Delian League*, instead the island allied itself with the opposing Peloponnesian League, led by Sparta. During the Peloponnesian War between the two leagues (*431 - 404 B.C.*), the Athenians took Thira and held it until the naval Battle of Aegospatami in 404 B.C., when the Spartans totally destroyed the Athenian fleet. The defeat resulted in Athens relinquishing to Sparta its considerable economic and political influence in the Aegean and the forced cessation of democracy in that city-state.

During the Hellenistic Period (*323 - 31 B.C.*), due to its strategic position in the Aegean, Thira became an important trading centre and naval base for the ruling Ptolemies of Egypt. In 31 B.C. the opposing Roman forces of Octavian and those of Mark Antony and Cleopatra met at the Battle of Actium. The resulting victory by Octavian's forces led the Roman senate to appoint him as the first Roman Emperor and subsequently to Thira being absorbed into the new Roman Empire.

Under Rome and onwards

Under Roman domination Thira was initially used as an open prison for dissidents exiled from Rome, but as the empire realised the island's strategic importance, Thira once again became an important trading centre in the Aegean.

In 330 A.D. when Emperor Constantine moved the centre of political power from Rome to Byzantium, renaming it Constantinople, Thira became part of the Byzantine Empire.

During the Christian Crusades (*1095 - 1291 A.D.*), the Franks (*from what is now West Germany*) settled on the island making the fortress of Skaros their capital. Constant disputes between the different factions within the Franks, Turkish aggression, pirate raids and attempts by Byzantium to retake the island, meant that this period of the history of the island was one of conflict and upheaval.

In the 13th century, Thira was absorbed into the Duchy of Naxos. The duchy was created in 1207 by the Venetians as a way of increasing their influence and economic power in the Aegean. It was at this time that the island was renamed Santorini, after Saint Irene, a Christian martyr of the 3rd century A.D.

The Venetian occupiers brought the Roman Catholic religion to Santorini, and for following centuries, Catholics and the original Orthodox population of the island co-existed more or less in harmony. Evidence of this religious freedom is found in some of the churches on the island built during this period that feature dual altars, one for Orthodox, and one for Catholic services.

As political instability and piracy in the Aegean declined, the island again acquired its own fleet and the economy improved.

In 1579, the island fell under Turkish occupation and became part of the Ottoman Empire. During this period the prosperity of the island continued to improve, confirmed by the fact that in 1821 the fleet of Santorini was the third largest in the Aegean, at 5,000 tons.

The island finally gained its independence in 1821 and joined the Greek Republic in 1830 after the signing of the London Protocol.

In 1939 at the beginning of the Second World War, Greece was invaded by Italy. However, the Greek army routed the Italians and drove them back to the Albanian mountains. To save face and for strategic reasons, Germany as allies of Italy, diverted forces to aid the Italians and in 1940 the Axis forces defeated the Greek army and occupied the country. The Greeks suffered enormously under the German administration, both through starvation and severe restrictions. Later the Germans handed the administration over to their allies the Bulgarians, who's military and political authorities continued the severe treatment of the local population, until in November 1944 the Axis forces in Greece surrendered.

The Greek civil war (*1946 -1949*) posed as the first example of a post-war communist insurgency in Europe. The victory of the anti-communist government forces led to Greece's membership in NATO and helped to define the ideological balance of power in the Aegean during the Cold War.

For those interested in history I have included a timeline of Greek and Roman events at the back of the book.

* *The Delian League was a confederation of some Aegean city-states led by Athens, which was formed primarily to counter threats from the Persian Empire. The leagues treasury was based on the island of Delos hence its name.*

Greek historic periods (*B.C.*)

Archaic   800 - 480
Classical   480 - 323
Hellenistic   323 - 31

Mythology

Deucalion and Pyra

The story of Deucalion is a story similar to the biblical account of the flood. According to Greek mythology, Zeus decided, with the help of Poseidon (*the Greek god of the sea*), to destroy humanity by flood, because he was tired of their sinful ways.

However, King Deucalion and his wife, Pyrrha, found favour with Poseidon and he arranged to spare them. Deucalion and Pyrrha were told in dreams to build a boat that would allow them to survive the imminent flood. After the deluge, they travelled in their boat until they came to a place called Parnassus, where they made sacrifices to Zeus. Zeus, upon seeing the sacrifices, sent Hermes the messenger god, to grant them whatever they wished for.

As the flood had destroyed all mankind, Deucalion and Pyrrha wished that they should not be left alone on Earth. Zeus hearing their request, ordered them both to cast stones onto the ground, the stones thrown by Deucalion became men, and those thrown by Pyrrha became women.

In the biblical story, Noah's sons become the founders of specific racial identities; in the story of Deucalion the same theme is present. Deucalion and Pyrrha have two sons, Hellen and Amphictyon, and two daughters, Protogenia and Melantho. Hellen founded a town, Hellas, in Thessaly, whose inhabitants became known as the Graeci or Greeks, and later became known as the Hellenes.

Another similar ancient myth about a flood, relates to the angry reaction of Poseidon, when Athena defeated him in their rivalry over the domination of Athens. Poseidon in revenge flooded the whole of Attica.

These myths are chronologically placed to around the time of the Minoan eruption. It is therefore credible that these stories could be an attempt, by the people of that period; to explain the reason for the catastrophic tsunami that followed the eruption, in cultural and religion-based terms of the day.

Culture

For those who have not visited Greece before, how can I explain the Greek people and their culture? It could be said that their way of life reflects many of the positive attributes of the UK in the not so distant past. These include a greater reliance and respect within the community for the family as well as the individual, a belief that the quality of life is more important than the quantity and a stronger self-reliance, rather than an increasing dependence on the state.

All I will say is that I find the Greeks, especially on the islands, sincere and extremely friendly and one of my greatest hopes is that the ever-increasing exposure to the tourist trade does not devalue, or corrupt these virtues.

Many of the locals have two separate lives, the first during the holiday season, working in one of the many service industries dedicated to the tourist industry. Then once the tourists have left, another that is more reminiscent of the past life on the island, which includes amongst others agriculture, fishing and community services.

You will find that, as in many Mediterranean countries, much of the day-to-day activities start very early then stop at lunchtime and reconvene early evening, continuing late into the night. So expect many of the shops and other services to be closed for a few hours in the afternoon. Remember the old adage "only mad dogs and Englishmen go out in the midday sun". I can confirm though there are no mad dogs, you will see a few that appear to be stray, but the majority have owners who let them out to wander free during the day. All in my experience are very friendly and pose no risk.

During your stay, one of the simplest ways of saying thank you (*Efkaristo*) is to take time to learn a few basic Greek words and phrases. I can assure you that even though the majority of Thirans in the main tourist areas speak at least a little English, your attempt to speak their language, if only a few basic words, will be much appreciated. To that end, I have added a glossary of frequently used Greek words and phrases at the back of the book.

Beyond the tourist

With the first drops of rain another summer season comes to a close. The days get shorter and the sunsets are a deeper red and purple. The Meltemi winds (*the Aegean equivalent of the French Mistral*) appear even stronger in the evenings. There is a fresher feel in the air; reminding all on the island that the summer is over.

The warm sunny weather continues for the whole of September and into October. The first fallen leaves bring a new urgency, the tourists may be leaving but this is a busy time for the islanders, who return to many of the trades that have been replaced in the summer by tourism.

Only in December can the people of Santorini slow down and start preparing for Christmas.

Winters on Santorini are mild, with temperatures dropping to around 10°C during January and February. Showers can be expected between October and May, with December tending to be the wettest month, rainfall is almost non-existent after March. The sun continues to shine during the winter, with Santorini still receiving roughly 4 to 5 hours a day during this time.

Cultural events

A number of cultural events and festivals are staged by the islanders during the year. I have included the details of two of the main national celebrations and the dates of other local festivals.

Epiphany

On the stroke of midnight on January 5th, the twelve days of Christmas officially come to an end. The 6th, known as Epiphany, has a special significance in Greece and one of the age old ceremonies which takes place on this day is the blessing of the sea and the local boats.

The modern observance at Piraeus, the ancient and modern port of takes the form of a priest hurling a large crucifix into the sea. Young men then brave the cold water and compete to retrieve it. These days, the cross is generally attached to a long chain, just in case that year's group of divers are less than proficient! After the diving, local fishermen bring their boats to be blessed by the priest.

The reason for the ceremony is that a tradition in the Greek Orthodox Church states that it was on this day that Christ was baptised by Saint John, and hence the connection with water.

At Epiphany, the Kallinkantzari (*malicious spirits*) who are said to be active during the twelve days of Christmas, are believed to be banished for the rest of the year.

Epiphany is also called the Phota or Fota, in reference to the day being a *Feast of Light*, and it is also the saint's day for Agia Theofana. While the biggest observance is at Piraeus, many islands and villages offer smaller versions of the event. It is definitely still a traditional holiday, performed by Greeks for Greeks.

The observance itself may pre-date Christianity. There was a ceremony around this date during the Roman period, to mark the opening of the maritime season. However, as any Greek fisherman will tell you, whatever the date of the opening of the maritime season really is, it definitely is not January 6th, as the inherent weather can still be stormy and uninviting.

The 6th is also said to be the approximate date of another festival held in the Roman period, during which emperors were worshiped. An ancient pagan festival was also held at this time, when it was customary to give precious offerings to the sea, river and spring spirits to assure their benevolence.

Easter

Easter in Greece does not always fall on the same date as that in most countries, as the Greek Orthodox Church uses the ancient Julian calendar, rather than the Gregorian calendar. In 2018, Orthodox Easter Sunday falls on 8th April. Easter is the holiest of

Greek holidays, and, as in other Christian traditions, it is also a celebration of spring.

At Easter in Greece, people leave the cities to spend the holiday in the countryside, many in their ancestral villages. However, Santorini is one of the very popular alternative destinations for Greeks to spend a traditional Easter. Food, of course, is central to the festivities, but not all Greeks eat the same Easter meal. The traditional Easter fare varies regionally, although all over the country it mirrors the same age-old wisdom that nothing should be wasted. Regional Greek Easter dishes include fresh herbs and tender young greens, dill, wild fennel, lemon balm, lettuce, sorrel and spinach. The meat chosen is usually lamb or goat; traditionally on Santorini it is goat.

One of the traditions of Greek Easter is to dye hard-boiled eggs red to signify the blood of Christ. At Easter, friends and family rap their egg against each other's, to see whose egg will survive un-cracked whilst saying in Greek, "Christ is risen" The other person says, "He is truly risen". This continues around the table until only one un-cracked egg is left. The owner of the egg being seen as blessed with luck for the forthcoming year.

Folklore and religious celebrations

Many religious events are continued, or have been revived, not only in respect for the history and religious beliefs of the islanders, but also as attractions for the tourists who visit Santorini.

Feast of Ipapandi	2nd February	Finikia and Oia
Easter Sunday	8th April (*Greek Orthodox*)	
Feast of Agios Epifanios	12th May	Akrotiri
Feast of Agios Theodosia	29th May	Fira
Feast of Agios Anargyros	1st July	Megalochori

Feast of the Prophet Ilias	20th July	Fira
Feast of Agios Ioannis	24th July	Monolithos
Epta Paidion	4th August	Oia
Feast of the Saviour's Metamorphosis	6th August	Akrotiri
Feast of Koimiseos of Panagia	15th August	Akrotiri
Feast of Panagia Episkopis (*the major Saints' day*)	15th August	Episkopis Gonias
Feast of Dormition of the Virgin Mary	15th August	Megalochori (*major festival*)
Feast of Agios Ioannis	29th August	Perissa
Feast of Panagia the Giatrissa	21st September	Thirassia
Feast of Panagia Mirtidiotissa	24th September	Kamari
Feast of Osios Averkios	22nd October	Emborio

Most of the above are celebrations on the day of the particular church's patron saint. These often include open-air markets selling traditional products, food and wine.

The Ifaisteia festival takes place in September and includes cultural events and concerts, culminating in an amazing volcanic firework display in the caldera. In 2018, the display will be on the 15th.

The Santorini Jazz Festival is held in July and the International Music Festival is held in early September, when famous artists from all over the world perform at the conference centre in Fira.

Dates of festivals can change, so please check our 'Santorini News' page on our website, for news of events and tourist attractions.

Local products

Santorini has a fertile volcanic soil. Cultivated carefully over the years, this soil has made Santorini well known for its horticultural and viticulture products.

Cheese

A brand of cheese called Chloro is made from goat's milk that is dried and matured in brine. It is usually grated and used as an addition to dishes.

Fava

Fava beans (*split peas*) are a main crop on Santorini. These are legumes, smaller than a pea, but from the same family. They make superb dips and other appetizers, but they're also great in salads, sauces, sautés, stews, pastas and risottos. The island exports the beans to many countries around the world.

Grapes

On Santorini, the predominant grape variety is Assyrtiko that produces both a very dry white and a dessert appellation wine. The predominance on the island of volcanic ash, lava and pumice, has created the perfect soil conditions for the Assyrtiko vines and from these the very distinctive wines of Santorini. The main vineyards are situated near the village of Megalochori.

The island's vintners cultivate the vines in low basket shaped crowns; the grapes are trained to grow within the baskets to protect them from chilling winds. Due to the lack of water on the island, the vines obtain most of the water they need from the nocturnal sea mist and this, together with the fresh northerly winds, provides the excellent growing conditions for the grapes that make the superb Santorini wines.

The dessert wines from Santorini are called Vinsanto, a derivative of the name Santorini. Vinsanto can be naturally sweet or fortified and must be barrel-aged for a minimum of two years. It is distinguished by its superb velvety palate with aromas of Crème Brûlée, chocolate and dried apricots.

Katsouni

Katsouni is a type of cucumber, but is longer, thicker, a lighter colour and is sweeter than its better known cousin.

Pumice

Santorini used to export pumice stone, but as a measure to protect the caldera, the quarries were closed in 1986.

Tomatoes

A variety of tomato plant has been developed by the farmers on the island to cope with the lack of water. It produces tasty sweet cherry tomatoes that are both sold for eating and used in the manufacture of *Belte*, the famous concentrated tomato paste.

White eggplant

White eggplant (*white aubergine*) is a traditional crop of Santorini. The plant was originally introduced from Egypt during the period when pumice was exported to Suez for the construction of the canal. Due to the soil and climatic conditions, it is not bitter like other eggplants, being instead, sweet and juicy. Capers, courgettes and watermelon are also grown on Santorini.

Crafts

Folk art

Weaving, painting and pottery are some of the many traditional folk arts to be found on the island. In the gift shops you will also find souvenirs made from pumice and the local volcanic stone.

Wine

As wine is such an important part of the economy on Santorini, it merits a special mention. The history of viticulture on the island goes back many millennia, as evidence found at the ancient site of Akrotiri confirms.

The uniqueness of Santorini wines comes from a number of factors, the volcanic soil, the micro-climate on the island and the varieties of grape grown. Although the area under cultivation is approximately 4,000 acres, due to the low rainfall, the yield per acre is relatively low. Total grape production lies between 1,500 and 4,500 tons, which translates into a wine production of between 1,050 and 3,150 tons per year. There are 36 different varieties of grape grown on the island. However, only 4 - 5 varieties are represented in the main wine production.

The vintage on Santorini takes place at the end of August and is a perfect time to visit the wineries.

Red grape varieties

The variety of red grape known as Mavrotragona is indigenous to the island and is used in the manufacture of a rich red high alcoholic wine, which is high in tannins and of medium acidity.

Mantilaria produces a deep red coloured grape that consequently produces a rich bodied wine and medium alcoholic nature.

Red wines

Mavrathiro is a barrel aged sweet dark red wine.

Caldera is a dry red wine.

Brousko is a dry red, white or rosé wine.

White grape varieties

The most abundant variety used in white wine production is Assyrtiko, accounting for 80% of the total production. The variety produces a strong-bodied wine that has a high acidity with metallic characteristics.

A second variety is Athiri. This vine, of Cretan origin, is used with Assyrtiko grapes to create a style of white wine, which has a strong aroma.

The Aidani variety is used in the production of the dessert wine Vinsanto to add aroma to the wine.

White wines

The most famous white wine on Santorini is Nykteri, derived from the Assyrtiko vine. The wine is barrel aged and has a characteristic metallic taste and high acidity.

Santorini is a fresh, dry white wine.

Assyrtiko wine, derived from the grape of the same name, is of high acidity and with a metallic element.

Vinsanto is a honey coloured sweet wine with a flavour of figs, raisins, and plums, made from grapes dried in the sun. There is also a Vinsanto sweet red wine.

Mezzo is a less sweet version of Vinsanto. The wine, which has a high acidity, has a flavour of peach and a lingering aftertaste of wildflower honey.

On page 53 I have detailed a number of wineries that are open to the public to learn about their production processes and of course to taste the finished product!

Local animals

Birds

There is a wide variety of bird life on the island, including the common sparrow, finch, raven, crow, swift, martin, collared dove, lark, little owl, and an impressive variety of birds of prey, which include kestrel, falcon, eagle, honey buzzard and sparrow-hawk. Marine birds include yellow-legged gulls, shearwaters and shags.

Dogs and cats

There are fewer cats on Santorini than most Greek islands, those there are, are outnumbered by the local dogs who wander free. The majority of the dogs have owners, but they are allowed to wander free during the day. Whether part feral or owned, the dogs are very friendly and pose no problem, except that is for taverna staff who tend to chase them off for the sake of their diners.

Dolphins

Although dolphins are to be found in the whole of the Mediterranean, they are a rare sight in open waters. However, recently a pod was seen to play in the bow wake of the ferries travelling to and from Santorini. So keep an eye out, you may just be lucky.

Donkeys

Horses, donkeys and mainly mules were the only means of transportation in Santorini up to the 1960's. They are part of the native charm and a symbol of Santorini. Today we can find them mainly at Skala Gialos, the old port of Fira, where during the summer they carry tourists up and down the endless steep steps that connect Fira to the small port below. They are extremely adept at negotiating the steps, but beware they do have a tendency to go fast!

Hummingbird?

During your visit, you may see a tiny flying creature that can easily be mistaken for a Humming Bird. In fact, this will most likely be a Hummingbird Moth, which is native to the island. Sadly Hummingbirds are only found in the New World.

Sheep and goats

Whilst sheep and goat rearing is not a major farming activity on Santorini, on your travels you will see large numbers, especially goats, as the resulting meat and milk is an important addition to the islands food production.

Poultry

Free-range chickens are reared on the island and one thing I can say, having been used to factory-farmed varieties in the UK, is that they taste wonderful, especially when they are cooked on a rotisserie in the Greek way.

Wild animals

For those interested in wildlife (*the animal type*), I have added the following information:

Apart from the odd feral goat and cat, wild mammals are scarce and inconspicuous on the island. Especially at night, the occasional brown rat can be seen scurrying across the road, or scavenging near to waste bins. At dusk, bats can be seen swooping through the evening sky feeding on the myriad of insects. The occasional dead hedgehog on the road, especially in the east, bares testament to their presence and in addition, stone martens and brown hares have also been seen on the island.

Greece reportedly supports ninety-five species of land mammals and research shows that Santorini shares in this diversity. Research has identified a distribution of twenty-five species of rodent around Greece. Just four species in total have been reported from the Aegean islands, namely the lesser mole rat, the broad-toothed field mouse, the brown rat and the house mouse.

Getting there

Package holidays

The first and obvious way of visiting Santorini is by booking through a tour operator. The major UK companies that are offering holidays on Santorini in 2018 are in alphabetical order:-

British Airways Holidays
Co-operative Travel
easyJet Holidays
Kuoni
Olympic
Thomas Cook Group
TUI

A la Carte

Most if not all of the major tour companies also offer flight-only alternatives and to give you an idea, the cost of a return flight from the UK into Santorini airport during the summer season, start from around £150 per person.

A second alternative is to fly direct to the island with easyJet or British Airways. A third alternative is too fly into Athens with BA, easyJet, or Ryanair and get a connecting flight to Santorini with Aegean, or Athens Airways. With this alternative, you can add a short stay in Athens to your itinerary. The flight time from Athens is about 45 minutes. The facilities at Santorini National Airport have recently been upgraded with new check-in-counters, conveyer belts, escalators and passenger facilities.

A final alternative is to fly into Athens and then take a ferry to Santorini. For example, one new service connects the port of Rafina, Athens and Santorini. Flying Car 3 by Hellenic Seaways is offering the service, which departs at 07:30 from Rafina and arrives in Santorini at noon. The return ferry leaves Santorini at 12:20, arriving back in Rafina at 17:10.

The latest airline information can be found on our website.

Hotels, studios and apartments

As you can appreciate there is a vast selection of holiday accommodation on the island, from pure luxury such as the Andronis Luxury Suites in Oia, boutique style hotels such as the Amerisa Suites in Fira, all the way down to basic studios.

Whilst I could write a book just on accommodation, my advice would be to first decide on the resort that suits your needs. As they say, one of the most important points is "location, location, location." If you want that quiet relaxing holiday, you don't want to be above a taverna and if you like the nightlife, you don't want to be in the middle of nowhere! Once you have decided on the resort you can search the web by entering, for example, 'hotels in Fira, Santorini'. There are a large number of hotel agency websites that offer the full range of accommodation on the island for you to choose from. Once you have your short-list, it is always advisable to check the hotels against review websites such as Tripadvisor.

One point I believe is less important is for your accommodation to offer a restaurant service. One of the joys of Santorini, is to visit the vast choice of tavernas and restaurants on the island and enjoy what can invariably be attractive surroundings and good food. Who wants to frequent a hotel restaurant, when you can sit by the sea and watch the sun set over the caldera. If you have a family, you will find that the Greek culture is very family orientated and therefore children are welcomed and catered for by restaurant staff. Many tavernas offer breakfast, either continental or English.

One thing I can confirm is that without exception, the accommodation I have stayed in within Greece in the last 30 years has always been clean and good value for money. You may find that at the budget end of the market, things can be a bit basic as far as room facilities are concerned. The top end of the market is as good as anything you will get back in the UK or US and for less!

Most 'self-catering' apartments and studios will have at least a two-ring stove, a fridge and basic cutlery, pots and pans and utensils, a double or two single beds with side cupboards and a wardrobe.

Usually there is only a shower with a W.C. For those who like a good night's sleep, it may be advisable if you are visiting in the high season, to select accommodation that has air-conditioning. In-room telephones and televisions are usually only to be found in the more expensive accommodation.

Insider tip: If you are not staying in 'self-catering' accommodation, many hotels and apartments have rules against meals being prepared and eaten in the rooms. I would also advise that where it is acceptable, it is courteous to dispose of any food waste yourself, and not to leave it for the hotel cleaning staff.

One strange but positive anomaly I have noticed in the past is that room cleaning and laundry changes occur more regularly than is specified in the brochure or room information. You should also find that when the odd problem such as a blocked sink or faulty light arises, raising the issue with the management will invariably result in a quick solution.

An alternative to booking before you leave home is to take a flight to Santorini and look for your accommodation when you arrive on the island. You will find there is always some accommodation available and at most times you can negotiate a good price.

The days of locals putting out a vacancy sign are all but over. If you arrive independently by ferry you will likely be met by Kamakis, which means harpoon, a very fitting name for the touts who get paid by the hotels for each guest they introduce. In Fira, as with the other main resorts, there are a number of property companies and travel agencies who may have suitable accommodation on their books, or at least will point you in the right direction. Some of the agencies buy room space in advance (*called commitment*) to achieve better rates and therefore increase their income. It is therefore advisable to shop around, as some will offer bargain prices at certain times, since they would rather put you in a pre-paid room, than leave it empty and lose money.

Camping

For those who enjoy the *back to nature* style holiday, or are looking for a budget way of visiting Santorini, there are two campsites on the island. The sites are well laid out with shaded areas to set up your tent.

Santorini camping and bungalows

Contact: Giorgos Gioulis
Fira
84700
Santorini
Phone: +30 22860 22944 and 22860 25064
Fax: +30 22860 25065
The site is 350 metres from the centre of Fira.

Facilities include:

24 hour hot water
Swimming pool
Pool bar
Mini-market
Self-service restaurant
Left luggage lockers and safe-deposit boxes
Kitchen facilities
Washing machine and ironing centre
Special sleeping bags areas
Rent a bed tent and rent a tent
Currency exchange, post and telephone services
Excursion booking
Wake up service
Free transfer from the port (*high season*)
Internet service

Perissa Camping

Contact: Galanakis Evagelos
Perissa

84703
Santorini
Phone: +30 22860 81343

Perissa Camping is located at Perissa beach.

Facilities include:

A taverna next to the beach
Beach bar
Mini-market
Left luggage lockers and safe-deposit boxes
Special sleeping bags areas
Rent a bed tent and rent a tent
Tourist office that provides: currency exchange, post and telephone services
Excursion booking
Free transfer from the port
Internet service

Places of interest

Places of interest on Santorini (*in alphabetical order*)

- Attractions for that rare rainy day, or to chill from the sun.

Akrotiri

In the southwest peninsula of the island is the archaeological site of Akrotiri. Due to a serious accident in 2005, the site was closed to the public for 6½ years. The site re-opened in April 2012 after extensive re-development, including the addition of improved visitor facilities and a bioclimatic roof that covers the whole site.

It was in the 1860's that the remains of the ancient town were found by workmen quarrying volcanic ash for use in the construction of the Suez Canal. However, it wasn't until 1967 that academic excavations started at the site, under the direction of the late Professor Spyridon Marinatos. The professor died in 1974 and it was his wish to be buried at Akrotiri on the site of his most important discoveries. The discoveries since 1967 have positioned Akrotiri as one of the most important archaeological sites in the Mediterranean ranking in importance alongside Pompeii and Herculaneum in Italy. Only the southern tip of the large town has been uncovered, yet it has revealed complexes of buildings, streets and squares, with remains of walls standing as high as 8 metres, all entombed in the ash deposited during the Minoan eruption.

The first habitation at the site dates from the Late Neolithic times (4th *millennium B.C.*). During the Early Bronze Age (3rd *millennium B.C.*), a sizeable settlement was founded and from the 20th to the 17th century B.C., the town developed into one of the main urban centres and ports in the Aegean. It is at this time that Santorini is believed to have become one of the most important trading partners of the Minoans*, who were centred on Crete and may even have been one of their colonies. The islanders cultivated olive trees and cereals, and reared a range of domesticated animals. They lived in highly advanced houses, many of three-storeys, some even with balconies. The town's design and infrastructure included innovations many centuries ahead of their time, such as an advanced drainage system.

The town

The area of excavation is large (*200,000 square metres*), but incredibly this is only approximately 4% of what is thought to remain of the town (*map on page 171*). There are therefore decades of further excavation to undertake and work on the site is ongoing.

The re-development of the site included the incorporation of a raised walkway, allowing visitors to view the archaeology from above, although there are a few areas where you can descend to the original ground level to get a true feeling on this amazing site. Entry is at the southern end of the site near to the paved ancient main street, where you will see the storerooms or warehouses of the ancient commercial city. During excavation in this area, a large number of Pithoi (*large terracotta jars*) were found and have been left in place. These still contained traces of olive oil, fish, and onions that were stored in the buildings.

The wide variety of imported objects found in the buildings, indicate the considerable contact the islanders had with other cultures. There are artefacts from Crete, the Greek mainland, the Dodecanese, Cyprus, Syria and the animals portrayed in many of the frescoes such as antelope, monkeys, and wildcats confirm contact with Egypt and North Africa. Furthermore the discovery of a loom-workshop, suggests that textiles were one of the exports from the island.

The site was not a palace-complex such as those found on Crete, but its technologically advanced piped fresh water system, flushing toilets (*the latter being the oldest such convenience discovered anywhere*) and fine frescoes, confirm that this was not a conglomeration of low-status dwellings. The frescoes were originally removed to the National Archaeological Museum of Athens, for safekeeping. Some though have been returned and are displayed in the Museum of Prehistoric Thira in the centre of Fira.

The frescoes discovered so far include amongst many scenes, one showing *Saffron-Gatherers* offering their crocus-stamens to a seated lady, perhaps a goddess; another with two antelopes, painted with the kind of confident, flowing decorative style that one might expect in a Persian manuscript. There is also the famous fresco of *The Boxing Youths* (*as shown on the title page of this book*) and yet another depicting a flotilla of boats accompanied by leaping dolphins, with young women with parasols, relaxing in the boats. One further example, representing a festival, illustrates two ports, the left port depicts members of the general population dressed in skins and tunics, a symbolic lion runs overhead. The right, probably of Akrotiri, shows a more aristocratic theme, with at its centre, a fleet of sailing ships at sea, with playful dolphins swimming alongside.

To get a true sense of the scale and urban complexity of this town, go to the 'plaza', where you'll see two-storey buildings and a spacious open area. Imagine the scene 3,600 years ago of a bustling multi-cultural market place with islanders, traders and visitors from across the Mediterranean, going about their daily lives. All of this and the many other marvels on the site, leave the visitor with a feeling of awe and incredulity that this was created by a civilisation so distant in time.

Information boards and display cases with information in four languages, including English, are located at intervals along the visitor walkway.

Open 08:00 until 20:00, closed Mondays. Entrance fee is 5€.

The people
Archaeological evidence seems to confirm that the town's life was terminated when the inhabitants were forced to abruptly abandon certainly the town, and most likely the whole island, as a result of the seismic activity which would have been a precursor to the ensuing Minoan eruption. This theory is reinforced by the fact that as yet no remains have been found of the inhabitants of the town, as was not the case in Pompeii and Herculaneum. Further indications that the inhabitants heeded prior warnings include personal possessions that have been piled up outside houses and beds that have been pulled out into the street awaiting collection.

However, this confirms that the warning was insufficient to give the residents sufficient time to vacate the town completely, or they believed that they would return to reclaim their possessions at a later date. The following and catastrophic eruption of the entire volcano then released the debris that buried the town. Fortunately for archaeology, this burial in ash and pumice has protected the buildings and their contents as well as, if not better than, at Pompeii.

Due to the lack of any physical remains of the inhabitants, it is postulated that many, if not all the islanders, took to the sea to flee from the impending disaster. Sadly though, if the theories as to the size of the resulting tsunami are correct, they would have stood little chance of surviving anywhere on the shores of the surrounding Aegean islands. Recent research has also shown that a Pyroclastic Flow (*a collapsing ash column*) can 'skip' across the sea for considerable distances and with a temperature of up to 1,000 degrees centigrade; anyone fleeing in a boat and caught in such a flow would be instantly killed.

After the Minoan eruption, Santorini lay uninhabited for three centuries, whilst most likely the peoples of the Aegean lost their fear of the island and the ecosystem recovered. It is sobering thought that Akrotiri was partially sheltered from the main force of the eruption of the volcano centred in the caldera. If the evidence of the frescoes is correct, the main town on the island was situated right on top of the volcano and would have been vapourised by the catastrophic eruption.

* The term Minoan is a relatively modern name for the civilisation that inhabited Crete and it is presumed Santorini in the 2nd millennium B.C. It was coined at the beginning of the 20th century by Sir Arthur Evans, the English archaeologist who excavated Knossos on Crete. He believed he had found the site of the palace and labyrinth of the mythical King Minos and therefore named the people who built it the Minoans. As previously stated, we only have one contemporary name for this ancient civilisation and its people, the Egyptian term being the Keftiu, but sadly we still know very little about their culture.

Ancient Thera *(map on page 172)*

The site of Ancient Thera is located on Mesa Vouno mountain, at an altitude of 396 metres. Excavations began in 1895 and continued until 1903, directed by a German archaeologist, Baron Hiller Von Gartringen, who found many wonderful artefacts from the ancient city. The cemeteries on the northeast and northwest slopes were excavated by N. Zapheiropoulos from 1961 to 1982.

During its time, ancient Thera played host to Phoenicians, Dorians, Romans and Byzantines. Down the centre of the city runs "The Sacred Way" and on either side are buildings that include groups of houses, market places, public baths, theatres, sanctuaries, the residence of Ptolemy Euergetes, tombs of the Archaic and Classical periods and early Christian churches. The ruins you see today are from the Hellenistic and Roman phases of the city.

The main monuments are:

Sanctuary of Artemidoros
Founded by Artemidoros of Perge, the sanctuary is entirely hewn from the rock and contains engraved epigrams and inscriptions including the symbols of the gods worshipped here. An eagle for Zeus, a lion for Apollo and a dolphin for Poseidon. Also engraved is the portrait of the wreathed Artemidoros, the founder of the sanctuary. The whole structure is dated to the late 4th or early 3rd century B.C.

Agora
The agora's southern precincts were the commercial heart of Thera, with the city's administration being conducted in what is now the central area. In the Roman period the northern precincts were added, which included a portico, monuments and sanctuaries erected in honour of dignitaries of the period.

Royal Stoa
The Royal Stoa is situated in the southwest of the part of the agora and measures 46 by 10 metres. The stoa dates from the reign of

the Roman Emperor Augustus (*27 B.C. - 14 A.D.*) and consisted of a colonnade of Doric pillars supporting a tiled roof, the main entry point was from the agora. In the northern section there were statues of members of Caesar's family and on the west wall two inscribed slabs were added in 149 A.D. to record that the repairs to the portico were paid for by Kleitosthenes, a wealthy Theran.

Temple of Dionysos
Built in the 3rd century B.C., on an artificial terrace to the north of the Agora, this small Doric temple had a cella and pronaos. The facade and roof were constructed of marble, with local stone being employed for the remainder of the building.

Theatre
The theatre lies to the southeast of the Agora and was constructed in the Hellenistic period. In its original form it had a circular orchestra, but during alterations in the 1st century A.D. the stage was extended, replacing part of the original orchestra.

Southeast of the city
This precinct were utilised exclusively for religious activities and contained sanctuaries to Apollo Karneios, Hermes and Heracles. In the square, Gymnopaediae (*which were dances performed by nude boys*) were held in honour of Apollo Karneios. Engraved on the rocks are numerous inscriptions referring to both deities and youths dating from the Archaic to the Roman period. Near the Temple of Apollo are inscriptions that quote the names of men and boys who were involved in pederastic relationships (*see page 13*).

Sanctuary of Apollo Karneios
This 6th century B.C. sanctuary stands in part on an artificial terrace, with the remainder being hewn from the rock face. The temple comprises a pronaos and cella and a courtyard that comprises an underground cistern, the roof of which is supported by six large monolithic pillars. Next to the sanctuary is a small repository.

Grotto and Gymnasium of the Youths

Nearby the Sanctuary of Apollo Karneios is a rock hewn grotto, which was dedicated to the god Hermes and hero-god Heracles. In addition, a sanctuary to Egyptian gods was added in the 3rd century B.C. and from the 2nd century B.C., the area was the site for the 'Gymnasium of the Youths'. In the 1st century A.D., the Romans added baths to the gymnasium complex.

Necropolis of ancient Thera

The necropolis (*cemetery*) is located on either side of the roads that led to the north and south harbours of the ancient city, the modern villages of Kamari and Perissa, respectively. The graves excavated span from the Archaic to the Roman periods.

The site of Ancient Thera is open Tuesday - Sunday: 08:00 - 15:00, entrance fee: 2€. Closed Monday.

Insider tip: For those with a hire-car, the road that leads up to the site from Kamari is not for the faint hearted, or those who suffer from vertigo. The road snakes its way up the mountain with 31 hairpin bends, many shear drops and no safety barriers. The car park is below the site and from there you walk up the mountain to the entrance (approx. 20 minutes).

Alternatively you can now take a donkey ride up to the summit. The cost is 10€ per person and the donkey is led by a 'minder'. There is also a minibus service from the Kamari side of the mountain, which costs 10€ for the return journey.

In late 2014, a 'road train' tour to ancient Thera was inaugurated, but at the time of going to press, it has not been confirmed whether this will run in 2018. The 'road train' is based in Fira (*see page 98*).

Insider tip: We would advise that you wear good walking shoes when visiting Ancient Thera as the paths are rocky and uneven.

Note: Ancient Thera is spelt with an *e* rather than an *i* as in the modern official name of the island, Thira.

Archaeological Museum

Located near the cable car in Fira town, the Archaeological Museum is mainly dedicated to a collection of ceramics, including those known as "Thira ware" and many Archaic and Classical pieces. There are though some Hellenistic and Roman sculptures and portraits. In my view though, the presentation of the exhibits is poor and many lack even descriptive labels.

Open: 8:30 - 19:30, (*closed Monday*), entrance fee is 3€.
Tel.: 22860 22217

Cruise ship disaster

On 5th April 2007 the cruise ship **Sea Diamond**, carrying 1,195 passengers, hit submerged rocks in the caldera and sank early the next day. Sadly a French passenger and his daughter were unaccounted for and it is presumed that they went down with the ship. Thankfully all the other passengers and crew were rescued. She now lies bow up, between 62 and 180 metres down, directly below the Señor Zorba Mexican restaurant, 3km south of Fira town, where there is also a memorial plaque to the two lives lost.

In late October 2017, the Greek Shipping Minister, Panagiotis Kouroumblis, ordered that the wreck of the cruise ship 'Sea Diamond' should be raised. At the time of going to press, the plans and timing of this major salvage operation had not been confirmed.

Folklore Museum

The folklore museum of Emmanoula A. Lignos is situated in Fira. Prior to being developed as a museum, the property was a house built into a cave and dates from 1861. The museum contains a host of exhibits which present the folklore of the island and the lives of the Thirans throughout history.

Open: 10:00 - 14:00 and 18:00 - 20:00

Megaro Gyzi

Megaro Gyzi is a beautiful 17th century mansion-museum located in Fira. The museum is in the Halls of the Cultural Centre where the following six permanent exhibitions are located:-

- An exhibition of old Thiraic manuscripts, covering Santorini public life from the late 16th to the early 19th century.
- An exhibition of engravings and maps from the 15th to the 19th century.
- A collection of paintings of Santorini donated by renowned Greek artists.
- A collection of photographs of Santorini covering the period between 1930 and 1956.
- A collection of Santorini strata.

During the summer months, the centre hosts a number of cultural events such as concerts, music recitals, traditional dancing presentations and painting exhibitions. Details will be posted on our website during the season.

Open between May 1st and October 31st
Opening hours: 10:00 - 22:00 Mon-Sat. Sunday, 10:00 - 16:00
Entrance: 3€

Museum of Minerals and Fossils

Situated in the central square of Perissa, the museum has exhibits of minerals and fossils from both Santorini and further afield.

Museum of Musical Instruments

The *Museum of Ancient Byzantine and Post-Byzantine Musical Instruments* is housed in the Old Community Building in Oia. The museum's creation is the work of Mr. Christodoulos Halaris, a prominent musician who has studied the roots of Greek music and its evolution through the centuries.

Museum of Prehistoric Thira

Located in Fira near the square, the Museum of Prehistoric Thira is a must if you are interested in the history of the ancient town and island. Exhibits cover the period of inhabitation on Thira from Neolithic (*New Stone Age*) to the late Cycladic periods. Many exquisite artefacts from ancient Akrotiri as well as items from the inhabitants' daily use are on show, including some of the beautiful frescoes found in the buildings.

Open: 09:00 – 16:00, (*closed Tuesday*), entrance fee is 3€.
Tel.: 22860 23217

Naval Museum

Situated in Oia, the Naval Museum is housed in an old mansion and portrays the maritime history of the island and its inhabitants. There are many exhibits that include rare figureheads, old maritime equipment and models of ancient and modern Thiran ships.

Open: 10:00 - 14:00 and 17:00 - 20:00 (*closed Tuesday*)

Cultural Village

Housed in Pyrgos, the 'Cultural Village', **is** a modern museum complex that charts the history and traditions of the island. Special events are also held at the centre throughout the summer season.

Santorini Arts Factory

The Santorini Arts Factory, based in the 'Old Tomato Factory' in the village of Vlihada (Vlychada), is the venue for a range of events during the summer months, including concerts, painting and photographic exhibitions. Information on events will be posted on the 'Santorini News' page on our website.

Tower of Nimborio (*Emborio*)

During the Venetian occupation of the island (*1207 - 1579*), fortified towers called Goulades were built at Skaros, the capital during this period, and in Oia, Pyrgos, Emborio, and Akrotiri. The towers served both as strongholds for the feudal lords and as warehouses for agricultural crops. The need for such strongholds arose not only from the constant political turmoil of the period but also from the constant raids of pirates from North Africa that plagued the Mediterranean at this time. The towers had bells to warn the local population of any approaching raiding parties. The Tower of Nimborio at Emborio, built in the 15th century, is a good example of the design of these strongholds and is relatively well preserved.

Wine Museum

Situated in Vothonas on the road to Kamari beach, the Koutsoyannopoulos Wine Museum presents the history of wine making on the island from the 1660's to the present day. There are auto-guides and audio-visual effects and the visitor can watch the film *The History of Santorini*. The museum is located in a cave 8 metres underground and 300 metres long.

Open daily: 12:00 to 20:00. Tel.: 22860 31322

Wineries

Santorini is famous for its wine and therefore, whilst on the island, a visit to a winery should be on your itinerary. Too many to mention in detail, I have included below a list of some of those open to the public:

Canava Roussos - situated in Episkopi

Visitors are welcome at this traditional Kanava Roussos winery guiding them around the installations and explaining the methods of production.

Hatzidakis - situated near Pyrgos

Although probably the smallest winery in the world, Hatzidakis' wines have achieved international recognition for their individuality and quality. Santorini 2000 won the bronze medal at the 2nd International Wine Competition in Thessaloniki. Santorini 2002 won the silver medal in the International Wine and Spirit Competition that was held in London in 2003. The greatest award gained so far was the gold medal for Santorini 2003 at the World Wine Awards.

Sigalas - situated between Foinikia and Baxedes

Guests are given a tour of the winery where they are informed of all the stages necessary to produce the wines, and of course are offered the opportunity to sample the wines of the estate. The scenic location of the winery and the position of the wine tasting room overlooking the vineyard and facing the setting sun, makes this a perfect location to learn the secrets of Santorinian wines.

Gavala - situated in Megalochori

The Gavalas family has been exclusively engaged in traditional wine production since the end of the 19th century. In the last 30 years they have concentrated on introducing their superior quality wines to an ever growing and international marketplace.

Coach tours

If you prefer for someone else to take the strain, there are a number of guided bus tours that visit places of interest and attractions on the island. The local travel agents will advise you on the range and cost of the excursions available.

Insider tip: A 7-day universal ticket which will allow entry to all the museums and archaeological sites on the island is available (including return visits). The price of the ticket is 8 euro for adults, half price for children and is available at the island's official museum ticket offices.

Fira and the villages

Fira

The island's capital Fira clings to the edge of a cliff that is, in fact, the rim of the ancient crater. The town is 300 metres above sea level and about 800 metres broad. If you arrive by ship or take the excursion to Nea Kameni, there is a winding stairway of 580 steps that link the 'Old Port' (*Skala Gialos*) to the town above. As the donkeys take this route, watch out for their droppings! Alternatively you can either take a donkey ride, or as many prefer the modern cable car.

The cable car was installed in the 1980's prior to this the mule ride from the port had been a tradition on Santorini for centuries. The Swiss-made cable car, known as the **Teleferique**, was a gift from a wealthy Santorinian, Mr. Nomikos, who owns a shipping line and whose vessels are regular visitors to the island. The cable car has vastly improved the transportation of visitors and their luggage up the steep cliffs to Fira. However, the mule owners did not lose out completely, they struck a deal to supplement their reduced income by taking a percentage of the revenue from the Teleferique (*the cable car costs 4€ per ascent/descent*).

Insider tip: If you plan to use the Teleferique, it is best to avoid early morning and late afternoon, especially when there are a number of cruise ships anchored in the caldera. Long queues can form at the cable car stations when their passengers are visiting the island, or returning to their ships.

Fira is a comparatively modern town, with houses built mostly during the 19th century, when the old Venetian capital at Skaros was abandoned due to earthquakes. The architecture is an attractive jumble of Venetian and Cycladic styles, one of the only similarities between the two being the whitewashed exteriors. There are two **cathedrals** in Fira, one Catholic and one Orthodox, which attract a large number of visitors each year.

The impact of Aegean tourism has made itself felt in Fira, judging from the abundance of tavernas, hotels, discotheques and shops. It is the largest urban area on the island and acts as the central hub for the island's travel network and tourist facilities.

The town has a population of approximately 2,000 and it is a pleasure to stroll through the quaint and colourful cobbled streets, soaking up the charm of this pretty town and stopping for a coffee, or doing a bit of window-shopping for those souvenirs to take back home, but make sure you wear sensible shoes, the cobbles can wreak havoc on the soles of your feet.

Santorini is dramatic and stunning, an island whose cliffs seem to glow under the exceptionally clear light of day, but which at sunset glow red, evoking images of that catastrophic explosion more than 3,500 years ago. During the day the superb views from the cliff-edge overlook the two Kameni islands, the newest additions to the volcano. For the adventurous a visit to these islands is a 'must' to add to your holiday itinerary.

Athinos Port

South of Fira and within the caldera, Athinios Port is the main port for all ferry boat arrivals and departures covering the other islands and the mainland of Greece. As a major tourist destination Santorini has daily connections with Piraeus, Paros, Naxos, Ios and Crete. There are also three ferries weekly running to all other islands of the Cyclades. A switchback road leads up the cliff to the main Fira to Megalochori road. Buses for Fira meet all ferry dockings, even late at night and leave Fira for the port approximately 1 hour before ferry departures.

The villages (*arranged clockwise from Fira*)

Firostephani

Located north of Fira and really a continuance of the town, it also is perched on the edge of the cliffs. Once again from here you get stunning views of the caldera and volcano and there are a number of interesting churches to visit.

Imerovigli

Imerovigli is situated at the highest point on the rim of the caldera at over 300 metres above sea level. The village is a short walk from Firostephani and one of the villages that should not be missed during your vacation.

Beside the village is the **Castle of Scaros** that guarded the western entrance to the island from attacks and its defences were never breached during its 600-year life. It was at the castle in 1207 that the Venetian leader Marko Sanouthos, after conquering the island, raised his Standard and renamed the island Santorini, after Saint Irene. The village is well serviced by tavernas, restaurants, bars, shops, hotels and rooms to let.

Finikia

This is a small village just outside Oia, which preserves many of the architectural and social elements of old Santorini. The village offers a lovely setting for a casual walk to take in all the amazing colours and styles of the local houses.

One of the popular evening walks to take in the dramatic and famous Santorinian sunsets is near Finikia. Nearby there is a mountain who's summit is reached by a **beautiful coastal path** that leads to a couple of churches (*popular as venues to make those wedding vows*). It takes about an hour to reach the top, but not a hike for the weak at heart. It is a lovely walk at any time of day, but if you do decide to go to view the sunset, one tip is to take a flashlight for the return journey.

Oia

The traditional settlement of Oia (*pronounced eea*) is located on the northern tip of the island, high on the cliff-top and just 11km from Fira. Particularly popular with the honeymooners and couples as Oia is the setting for some of the most magnificent views on Santorini. The village is pedestrianised and criss-crossed by a myriad of winding alleyways and cobbled streets. With cliffs on one side and the sea on the other, the dramatic views add a further reason to visit this pretty and peaceful village.

The village square overlooks the sea and from here at sunset you can view and capture on your camera some fantastic sunset images. **Ammoudi beach** is directly below the village, accessible by a steep path down the cliff, or via the road.

The unique appeal of Oia lies in its village houses, many hewn out of the volcanic rock, with some whitewashed and others painted blue or ochre. There are also neo-classical mansions with their courtyards, narrow cobbled alleys and blue domes sparkling in the sunlight.

In 1900 the village had a population of close to 9,000. However, after the devastating earthquake of 1956 the population had dropped to just 500 permanent residents. The village has a strong maritime tradition and in 1951 Captain Antonis Dakoronia established a **maritime museum** in the village 🌥. Although like many other buildings, it was destroyed in 1956 earthquake, the museum reopened in 1979 and is open to visitors.

As in Fira, there is a cliff top walk which offers you breathtaking views over the lagoon and across the whole archipelago. Walk on and you come to the remains of an old **Venetian fortress**.

Oia has a cultural centre, many art galleries and a host of quality shops that sell handicrafts, jewellery and a vast array of souvenirs.

A map of Oia is not available due to the myriad of alleyways and lack of street names in Oia which would render a map almost useless if not actually confusing.

Vourvoulos

Vourvoulos is a traditional village, located 2.5km from Fira. Although the village is situated near to the capital, the beach of the same name is another 5km from Fira on the northeast coast. There are good tavernas and cafés as well as a bar and swimming pool.

Monolithos

Monolithos is a typical Santorini village, situated approximately 9km from Fira and near the airport. Details of the resort of Monolithos can be found in a following chapter on beaches.

Mesa Gonia (*Episkopi Gonia*)

Mesa Gonia is located about 6km from Fira near Kamari and has a pretty **Byzantine church** dedicated to the Assumption of the Virgin Mary. Built at the end of the 11th century, it was paid for by the Byzantine Emperor Alexios Komninos.

Emborio

Emborio is a larger village with small picturesque streets and pretty whitewashed houses. The village was one of a number on the island that had a **fortified tower** during the medieval period, remains of which are still visible north of the village. These strongholds called *Goulades* were primarily for the population to take refuge in during pirate raids and political unrest (*see page 52*).

Exomitis

Exomitis is both a cape and a village on the southern coast near to Perissa. On the rocks to the right hand side of the road from Perissa to Exomitis, are ancient tombs. On one of the tombstones is a carving of a huge viper, the 'Oxentra', which is ancient Greek for 'Oxia', the modern name for a viper.

Akrotiri

Akrotiri village is situated on the furthest south-western peninsula of the island about 12km from Fira. Excavations in the area discovered the town on the acropolis and a fortified Venetian castle, built during the medieval age, but destroyed after the occupation of Santorini by the Turks. There are two old churches in the village, **Agia Triada and Ipapandi tou Sotiros**.

Megalochori

The village of Megalochori is 9km from Fira and contains the **Churches of Agia Anargyri, Isodia tis Theotokou and Agios Nikolaos Marmaritis** on the road to Emborio, all worth a visit.

The church of Agios Nikolaos Marmaritis (*Marmaro is the Greek name for marble*) is interesting as it was built on the site of a 4th century B.C. temple and contains many Doric style features re-used from the previous pagan building.

Pyrgos

One of the prettiest villages on Santorini, it has some fine old houses, the remains of a **Venetian castle** on the hilltop (*worthy only for the 360° views of the island from its battlements*) and several Byzantine churches; the most notable is the Theotokaki, with some interesting frescoes.

The **Monastery of Profitis Ilias** lies 3km from the village. Located on the peak of the mountain of the same name, its construction started in 1771, with the help of the bishop of Fira, Zacharias, and the approval of the Patriarch of Constantinople (*the Greek Orthodox equivalent of the Roman Catholic Pope*).

After the Patriarch's spiritual protection for the monastery was pronounced, it was honoured by becoming a Patriarchical monastery. In the 19th century the monastery was expanded from its original form, when the King of Greece, Othon, impressed by its charm, ordered further construction and embellishment. The monastery's museum is full of ecclesiastical articles, including icons from 15th and 18th centuries, silver bound scriptures, and the diamond-adorned mitre of the Patriarch Gregory 5th. The monastery plays host to a fascinating religious feast on 20th July each year.

Pyrgos also houses the 'Cultural Village', a modern museum complex that charts the history and traditions of the island. Special events are also held at the centre throughout the summer season.

On Orthodox Good Friday, the village of Pyrgos will host an annual **illumination spectacular** as part of the celebration of Easter on the island. The old Venetian castle and the entire village will be lit up with lanterns, which create a dramatic and spiritual experience for the visitor.

Exo Gonia

Exo Gonia is a small traditional village, 7km from Fira. The village is quiet and unaffected by large crowds. Narrow streets, beautiful houses, open air cafes and a few tavernas make this a pretty village to visit. An old tomato paste factory has been transformed into a **cultural centre** that hosts various summer exhibitions.

Vothonas

The village of Vothonas is 6km from the town of Fira. It is one the most picturesque villages on Santorini. You can usually be assured of peace and quiet to walk and enjoy this quaint village carved out of rocks. Vothonas village is the architectural showpiece of Santorini island. There are many inspiring facades of houses that are conspicuous by their stylish doorways and pilasters that blend perfectly with the profusion of white domed houses.

A visit to Vothonas is incomplete without visiting the magnificent **Church of St. Anna** , which happens to be the oldest church in the village, being built in 1827. The main focal point in the church is the intricately carved wooden panel, depicting scenes from the Old Testament.

Messaria

Messaria is a very picturesque village, surrounded as it is by gardens and vineyards, situated 4km from Fira in the centre of the island to the southeast.

As the prime location of wine production on the island, Messaria has recently seen the development of luxury hotels and specialist shops. The **Churches of Metamorphosis tou Sotiros and Agia Irini**, both build between 1680 and 1700 and the **Church of Metropolis** are all worth a visit .

Messaria has a Cycladic charm with its picturesque white washed houses and tiny winding streets. One of the most impressive buildings in the village is the **Argiros Mansion**, built in 1888 by winemaker George E. Argiros, seriously damaged by the 1956 earthquake it has just recently been restored. It is a typical 19th century Santorini style home and if you are interested in architecture, it is worth a visit.

Karterados

Only 2km from Fira, Karterados is a traditional village built beside a ravine that was cut by a stream. Its existence is recorded back to the 17th century. The name of the village comes from the Greek word *karteri* meaning waiting point or ambush point, probably because ambushes were set to trap marauding pirates.

The original dwellings are cave houses built deep into the rock faces. During the 19th century, many of the captains of the island's boats lived in the village.

The village square has a traditional windmill and a memorial plaque to commemorate those who died in the Second World War. On the left hand side as you leave the square, the road curves sharply to the left, and there you will discover the **Steps of Galaios**. Barely visible from the main road this is a small neighbourhood of cobbled streets, captains houses and cave houses built into the rock.

Kodochori

An eastern suburb of Fira, the village contains some interesting architecture, **two wonderful mansions,** the **Church of Analipsis** and a **folklore museum** .

Villages that are also beach resorts are covered in the next chapter.

Beaches

The two main beach resorts on the island are Kamari and Perissa, with Kamari being the most popular. Mesa Vouno mountain divides the two beaches into separate resorts.

All the beaches are well served by bus routes from the central hub in Fira, starting early in the morning and continuing into the late evening.

I have arranged the main beaches clockwise starting north of Fira.

Symbols

- ① Restaurant facilities
- 🍸 Bars
- 🌊 Water-sports
- 🏖 Blue flag beach (*International quality beach award*)
- 🤿 Scuba diving

(*Beach facilities can change without warning, the following are correct at the time of going to press*)

Ammoudi and Armeni ① 🍸 🌊

Ammoudi and Armeni are two beautiful beaches, which are the main shorelines for those staying in Oia. Ammoudi is directly below Oia and reached by steps (*or a donkey ride*), or via the paved road down to the bay. The beach is rather stony and once you enter the sea there is a sharp incline to deep water, beware when swimming as the currents can be very strong. The beach is also be affected by the wash from passing ships, so place yourself higher up the beach for safety. Armeni beach is a little further south.

Baxedes ① 🍸

Baxedes is the main beach at the northern end of the island. Located 3km from the village of Oia, Baxedes is a quiet beach, with the usual black volcanic sand, ideal for those who like to avoid the hustle and bustle of the more popular beaches. One drawback though is that this beach, as with all in the north, can suffer when the Meltemi wind blows. The beach is serviced by a few tavernas.

Koloumbo

Koloumbo beach is next to Baxedes, the beach is mostly made up of white pebbles. If there is a strong wind, this is one beach to miss. The beach is beautiful and quiet, but has no facilities. In November 2014, plans were announced to develop extensive harbour facilities outside the caldera at Koloumbo.

Pori ⑩

Another quiet beach, for those wanting to get away from the crowds, situated 10km from Fira. The red rocks of Pori beach make this a scenic venue for a relaxing beach day. Traditionally this is a small fishing port and therefore has few amenities. However, there is a traditional Greek taverna with quality fresh fish on the menu.

The beach is composed of black sand, but has no umbrellas or sun lounges.

Vourvoulos ⑩

Vourvoulos beach is a mere 7km from Fira, located on the northeast coastline. The beach is sandy with pebbles. In the right conditions, it is ideal for swimming and sun bathing, although there are few sun-beds available. The plus of Vourvoulos beach is that it is among the lesser-known beaches of Santorini and therefore you can achieve some privacy and peace.

Regrettably though, the beach is not as well maintained as others on the island and can be a little litter strewn. Also, when the Meltemi blows, sunbathing can be unpleasant and the seas can become very rough. In these conditions it is advisable when swimming, not to stray too far from the shoreline. At the far end of the beach there is a small fishing harbour and a taverna.

Monolithos ⓘ 🍴

Just north of Kamari and on the eastern coast is the beach of Monolithos, most popular with the locals. Here you will find more peace and quiet than other Santorini beaches, but with all the facilities of the other beaches including a number of tavernas for drinks, snacks and meals. The shallow wading waters make Monolithos Beach ideal for children, plus there is a playground and a volleyball area on the beach. The beach is composed of volcanic sand.

Kamari ⓘ 🍴 🔈 BF 🔈

If it's a beach resort you are looking for on Santorini, then Kamari is the place for you. The black sandy beach, at least 8km in length and of *Blue Flag* status, is the main attraction of Kamari. The main seafront is 2km long, consisting of hotels, restaurants, bars, discos and shops to please all tastes and budgets. In the day though, it can be quite sleepy and relaxed. A wide range of water-sports are also available such as water skiing, windsurfing and paddleboats.

Completely rebuilt after the 1956 earthquake, Kamari was the most important strategic point on the island after the decline of Akrotiri in ancient times.

Not far from the village is the archaeological site of Ancient Thera. Also of potential interest in Kamari is the **Church of Panagia Episkopi**, which was built in 1100 A.D. The best time to visit the church is on August 15th during the feast of the Virgin Mary, when the church celebrates with a large festival. You are invited to join in with the merry making, with plenty of food, dancing and singing taking place. If you are around on September 24th the **Church of Panagia Myrtidiotissa** celebrates with a festival, where again the tourists are invited to dine and wine with the villages.

Behind and parallel to the beach promenade is a street where you will find to the north end a shopping centre, a cinema and arranged along the street, shops, restaurants, tour and travel agents, the main bus stop and ATM's.

The town is connected to Fira by a half hour bus service until 23:00.

Perissa ⬤ 🔲 🔳 🔳 BF ♿

In the southern corner of the island is Perissa, known as another of the best beach resorts of Santorini. The beach is 7km long and composed of black sand, this coupled with the clear deep blue sea create a stunning setting that attracts thousands of visitors every year. Seafront tavernas, hotels, bars, discos, camping facilities and trees for shade, add to the beach's popularity. The road that runs parallel to the beach is open to traffic making it easy to visit the beach area. Towards the southwest is the beach of Agios Georgios, a quiet haven away from the frenetic main beach.

The beach offers the best water-sports facilities on the island with windsurfing, water skiing, pedalos and boats for hire as well as sub-aqua centres. The beach is also the location of the **SeaTrac** facility, which allows independent access to the sea for **disabled visitors**.

The **Byzantine Church of Agia Irini** (*Saint Irene*) is worth visiting and especially during August 29th and September 14th when festivals are held in honour of the patron saint of the island. Agia Irini died on the island while in exile in 304 A.D. Another attraction in the area is Ancient Thera, which is not far from Perissa.

Backpackers and the younger set seem to prefer Perissa Beach, which has the most affordable accommodation and facilities.

Perivolos ⬤ 🔲 🔳

Perivolos is very much the beach to see and be seen on with a number of lively beach bars. Directly behind the beach there are tavernas, shops, supermarkets, studios and apartments. Sports facilities are available on the beach, which is located on the southern tip of the island. The beach is composed of volcanic sand and black pebbles, hence its alternative name of Black Beach.

Agios Georgios Ⓘ 🚽 🗺

Located on the southern tip of the island, water-sports are available here. There are beach bars and a few tavernas can be found here, but the beach offers a perfect spot for those preferring a solitary swim avoiding the massive crowds. The beach is accessible from both Emporio 3km away and Perissa 3.5km away.

Vlichada (Vlychada, Vlihada) Ⓘ 🚽 🗺

Situated at the southwest end of the island, 13km from Fira, Vlichada is a very beautiful quiet beach and is a perfect spot for those wishing to avoid the big crowds. The long beach is composed of the usual volcanic sands and is sheltered by the cliffs behind. These have been eroded by the wind and sea to form small caves and an overall moon-like landscape, which adds to the strange but scenic attraction of this beach. Vlichada is the home of a number of companies offering both sailing and motor-boat hire services.

Red Beach Ⓘ 🚽

Not far from the ancient site at Akrotiri, is Red Beach (*also known as Kokkini Ammos*). You couldn't ask for a more breathtaking setting for a swim. Soaring red lava cliffs that form a backdrop to the black sandy shore, with a clear turquoise sea, all add to the very picturesque setting for that day on the beach. There are two restaurants and a nearby hotel that offer alternative venues for that lazy lunch. If you like excursions, boats leave from Akrotiri to other beaches further down the coast. Bus services run from Fira to the beach, a number of organised tours also stop at the beach and there is a car park a few minutes' walk away. One suggestion is combining a visit to Red Beach with one to the famous archaeological site of Akrotiri.

White Beach Ⓘ 🚽

White Beach lies in a cove next to Red beach. Similar to the Red beach with white pebbles on the beach, the enclosing cliffs are also white, giving the beach its name. This beach is only accessible by boat trip from Akrotiri (8€), or on foot from the Red Beach.

Insider tip: Be aware that if you take the boat trip to Red and White beaches from Akrotiri, the boat moors just off the beaches and you have to swim to the beach.

Cape Akrotiri ① ▮

There are a couple of quiet undeveloped beaches in the area, although they are a little difficult to get to. The cape's main claim to fame is the **Akrotiri Lighthouse**, which is one of the largest in Greece. Built in 1892, its light reaches 25 nautical miles out to sea. It was manned until 1988, but is now automatic. The lighthouse itself is not particularly enthralling, but the views from the point are well worth a visit.

Thermi

Black pebbles and pumice, red volcanic rocks, geothermal springs, the ruins of a small church and the baths that used to offer a natural Spa, this is Thermi. You may spot this beach if you take a trip around the caldera, but if you want to explore this fascinating area on foot, follow the cobbled road and then the path that descends below the "Ta Thermi" pizzeria, near Megalochori.

Make sure you visit the impressive small church of Hristos ta Thermi (Christ at Thermi), which is built into the volcanic rocks, next to the ruins of rock-hewn houses.

Insider tip: As the beaches are of black volcanic sand, in the height of summer the sand can become 'red-hot', so a good investment is to buy a pair of swin shoes. These are available in beach shops and large supermarkets and cost around 10€. They also protect the feet from sea urchins and sharp stones.

Insider tip: If you would like a day on a true sandy beach and also visit another island, you can take a ferry from Santorini to Ios. Ferries take about an hour and sail four times a day. Details can be obtained from most travel agents.

Activities

Organised trips

Most tour companies will offer a selection of excursions to their customers at the traditional "Welcome Meeting". These range from the sometimes-abused title of a "Greek Night", day boat trips around the caldera including a barbeque, spa days, to trips to the local wineries.

Many of the excursions can also be found independently, through the many tour companies situated in the towns on the island. Whilst the choice is down to the individual, before booking with your tour operator, I would recommend you shop around to see what offers are available and if possible talk to other holidaymakers who have already been on the tour in question.

Activities for the very young

If you have booked hotel accommodation through a tour company, most offer activities for the very young within the hotel precincts, these should be listed in the company's brochure.

Other than the obvious days on the beach, I will outline a choice of activities that are suitable for children.

In or near some of the main resorts you can usually find a limited number of fairground attractions for an evening treat including dodgem rides, toy train rides and mini-carousels.

Boat trips can be booked in most resorts, as can pedalo hire, banana rides and paragliding. The horse riding stables on the island also offer pony rides for the young, ask locally which is the nearest.

Most of the larger supermarkets and souvenir shops stock a wide range of toys, including such things as childrens' fishing kits, snorkelling sets and fun beach items, such as bucket and spades, lilos, toy dinghies, frisbees, beach balls, racket ball sets, etc.

Pubs, bars and adrenalin

Due to its size and diversity, Santorini lacks the all-out day party scene of Mykonos or Kos. However, being the third most popular tourist destination in the Dodecanese after Rhodes and Kos, Santorini has a vast selection of nightlife.

Most of the lively bars and nightclubs of Santorini are concentrated in Fira, it is the prime gathering spot on the island, the place where people begin and often end their nights. Dress codes do apply in some clubs. Many of the clubs and bars along the caldera cliff are renovated cave houses.

Clubs tend to be indoors or surrounded by high walls due to the strict noise abatement laws, whereas many of the bars, as they close earlier, can offer beautiful views of the caldera from their patios.

True to my word of being unbiased and independent, I will not comment on which is best or worst. The bars and clubs also cater for different tastes and therefore one seen as cool by one person could be totally un-cool to others.

To give you a flavour of the nightlife, I have outlined below a selection of the main venues and their facilities. My suggestion though, is to talk to the locals and those tourists who have already sampled what's on and make your own decision.

Bars

Fira and the other main resorts are bursting with bars and pubs and there's something to suit everyone. From the latest dance anthems to the cheesiest tunes, a great indie scene and a splash of funky house and R'n'B, the music is non-stop and the bars can get packed with revellers. Music is usually played until midnight, when if you still have the energy, the clubs take over.

The Tropical bar is a sophisticated euro tunes venue, with a wide bar counter *(ideal for dancing)* and a balcony with a spectacular view of the caldera. Friendly and social, it makes a great venue to start the night off as you mean to go on.

The Two Brothers Bar in Fira is a very lively bar. The brothers are generous with the shots and the DJ knows how to keep the revellers on the dance floor. It's somewhat hidden, just past the main part of town down an alley. Look for the sign over door.

Kastro Cafeteria, is located at the cable car entrance and offers both the facilities of a bar and taverna, with a great view of the volcano. The cool breeze and the comfy chairs are the perfect companion to parched throats and tired feet.

Other bars include: music style

Fira:

Art Café

Bar 33   - Greek

Café Del Mar

Casablanca   - soul

Classico café   - background

Ellenes   - Greek

Francos Bar   - classical

Highland Bar

Kira Thira Bar   - jazz/rock

Lava Café

Murphy's Bar	- mainstream
Remvi	
Select Café	- international
Tango Bar	- mainstream
Tithora	

Kamari:

Oxygen	- mainstream
Hook Bar	- 60'/70's
Mango Bar	- mainstream
Valentino's	- sophisticated
Aegean Café	- Irish style bar

Katrados:

Mojito Café	- background

Oia:

Bar 1800	- sophisticated
Oias Café Gallery	
Papagalos Café	
Pelekanos Café	- atmospheric
Zorbas	

Perissa:

Dorians   - 60/70's

Sea View   - mainstream

Perivolos:

Salty Beach Club

Wet Beach Bar   - mainstream

Chilli Beach Bar   - mainstream

Many people gather in Oia to watch the sunset. If you are then off to party in Fira, the Tropical Bar offers some spectacular views while you enjoy that early evening cocktail.

Clubs

As good as the bar-life is, if you want to go clubbing, holidays on Santorini will still live up to all your expectations. Bars are mostly free, but the clubs charge around 3 - 10€ entrance fee. Prices for drinks at the venues around the towns are quite reasonable, probably the same if not a little cheaper than back in the UK or US.

The club opening hours are:-

Sunday to Thursday: 0:00 to 04:00
Friday and Saturday: 0:00 to 06:00

Koo club is Santorini's most established club and the most famous night-time venue on the island. It is always crowded with revellers in a mood to dance and party, a testament to its popularity among tourists, locals and European celebrities.

It has a large outdoor patio in a tropical setting in contrast to the high-energy dance scene inside.

Enigma club was established in the summer of 1979. A large club with a great atmosphere and decorated with imposing arches, mood lighting, cushioned benches and a great dance scene. Outside there is a large seating area, ideal for relaxing between dances.

Dom club is one of the liveliest nightclubs and it is located in Kamari. With a cage on stage, the non-stop partying goes on until the very early hours.

Other clubs include:

Casablanca Soul	- Fira
Club 33	- Fira
Mamounia	- Fira
Town	- Fira
Question Mark Beer House	- Perissa

During the day, beach bars can be a great venue if you want sun bathing with a little extra entertainment. As Perivolos is very much the beach to be seen on, the two beach bars there, namely Wet and Chilli, are very popular with the clubbing fraternity during the day.

Adrenalin

There's so much to do and yet days can be as chilled out or action-filled as you like. For adrenalin junkies don't miss the speedboat trips and the many other exhilarating water and land-based activities. For the more laid back, relax and catch some rays, or visit the amazing archaeological site of Akrotiri.

Another option is to book a Jeep safari, you will find these advertised in the local tour company offices.

Dependent on the company, they either pick you up at your hotel, or from a convenient collection point. You will travel in a convoy of jeeps following an experienced guide over mountains, through volcanic landscapes and down dirt tracks to the coast. This is a great day out, taking in the lovely landscape of Santorini and its villages.

Lunch is organised along the route at either a taverna, or alternatively, a picnic or BBQ on the beach.

Insider tip: *Take plenty of sun-tan oil and some good protective clothing, with the jeeps being open to the sun, you can come back looking like a lobster and of course don't forget your driving licence!*

Visiting the Volcano

I have added this activity under the *Adrenalin* section as to be honest you will need a good supply to complete this trip. In my view though, to stand on the summit of a live volcano and take in the incredible moon-like landscape all around, the expenditure is well worth it.

These tours are offered by a cooperative of boat operators called the **Ships Joint Venture of Santorini** and depart from Skala Gialos (*the port below Fira*) Athinios Port and Ammoudi, below Oia. There are various tours to choose from, ranging from a simple boat trip to the volcano, to a combined boat and coach tour that takes in the volcano, Thirassia and sunset at Oia.

The tours can be booked at most of the travel agents in the towns and resorts. To give you an idea, *Tour 2* to the volcano starts at either 11:00 or 14:00 and departs from Skala Gialos, just below Fira. The cost is 18€ per person.

A traditional Caicque takes you first out to Nea Kameni, the youngest and still active (*but at present dormant*) volcano. A new landing stage, improved signage, seating and shaded areas were added on the island in early 2017. Once on the island, you take a cinder path past a number of previously active craters, finally reaching the summit and the latest addition to the list of volcanic vents.

Returning to the boat, it then moves on to Palea Kameni, where it drops anchor for those who would like to swim in the hot mineral springs that emanate from deep underground. The boat then returns you to the 'Old Port' for debarkation. The round trip takes roughly 3 hours.

If you book one of these tours and I do recommend them, then I would advise you to wear sturdy walking shoes, apply a high-factor sun cream, take plenty of fluids and a good hat. I know this will sound a bit excessive, but also add a parasol or umbrella, I am sure in the end you will find it invaluable. In the height of summer the volcano bakes and there is no vegetation, so the heat reflects off all the rocks and hits you from every direction.

One last point, if you are a good swimmer and would like to take advantage of the swim off the boat at Palea Kameni, take your own towel as these are not provided. The swimming stop lasts for about an hour, with those not participating staying on board. One word of warning though, the hot mineral waters can discolour jewellery and stain clothes (*although any stain should wash out*). To be safe, take any jewellery off and don't wear that favourite swimsuit!

Although the trip to Nea Kameni is an amazing experience, I would not recommend it for those with health issues, as the walk up to the volcano's summit is very strenuous, especially in high summer.

Sports and recreation

Sports and recreation

Banana boats and ringos

For those not conversant with this activity, a banana boat is a long thin inflatable with seats for the participants positioned down its length. The banana is towed behind a speedboat and the objective is to stay on and enjoy the ride. Ringos are an alternative to the banana and are large inflatable rings towed behind the boat. Banana and/or ringo rides can be found at all the main beaches. For safety it is important that you wear the life jacket supplied.

Boat hire

Small outboard boats such as RIB boats can be hired from some of the beaches on an hr/day basis. Larger sea going boats can be hired on the island on a daily or weekly basis. (see Perissa page 70 an Vliclhada page 71)

Cinemas

There are two cinemas on Santorini, one indoor and one outdoor, both screen the latest 'bockbusters'. I have given times, but it is always advisable to check with the cinema beforehand.

Cine Villaggio, Kamari - An indoor cinema with air conditioning. snack bar and refreshments.
Films start every evening usually at 19:30 and 22:30
Films are shown in original versions with Greek sub-titles.
Open all year round - tel : 22860 32800

Open Air Cinema - As the name implies it is open-air. Situated in a beautiful setting on the road to Kamari.
Films start every evening usually at 21:00 and 23:15
Films are shown in original versions with Greek sub-titles.
Open between June and September, tel: 22860 31974

Cycling

There are a large number of cycle hire shops on the island, so I suggest you ask at your hotel/apartments, they should be able to give you directions to the nearest. Bike hire charges range from 4 to 12€ a day, cheaper if you hire for several days. Cycles come with locks so you needn't worry about security, but beware, they all look the same, so it's a good idea to tie something on it, so you can spot which one is yours. One other tip is don't try to load a bike onto a local bus, they are not allowed.

Donkey rides

From the top of the cliff in Fira, there is a steep path that leads down to the port. Donkey rides are available from the top to the bottom and vice versa. However, if you want to experience the dramatic views of the caldera, I would suggest that the former of the two is the least un-nerving.

Insider tip: Beware of where you tread though, as the donkeys do tend to leave their mark on the path!

Our suggestion is to walk down to the port and take the Teleferique back up to Fira.

Fishing

Fishing is a popular pastime on the island for the locals, both by boat and off-shore, but for those visitors who would like to relax and try their luck with a rod and tackle, then most of the main resorts have a shop selling fishing tackle and bait. It is often the local hardware retailer or similar, that doubles up as a fishing tackle shop and although I am not an experienced fisherman, I have been surprised at the quality and range of gear on offer and the low cost of the items. To give an idea to the interested reader, a good extendable rod is around 25€.

The sea around the island abounds with a wide variety of fish, a fact that confirms the absence of pollution. The species include mullet, bream, blackfish, grey pandora, picarel and horse mackerel, with molluscs and crustaceans such as octopus and lobster.

Jet skis, Windsurfing and Paragliding

A wide range of water-sports are available in the majority of the beach resorts. However, I have found in the past that the specific facilities available can change from year to year and therefore it is not possible to give a comprehensive and accurate list at the time of going to press. Please refer to the chapter *Beaches and resorts* (*page 67*) for those that have water-sports facilities.

Red Bull's Art of Motion

Red Bull's Art of Motion competition returns to Santorini each year in early October.

The competition brings together the world's best freerunners who compete for the world title on unique courses around the globe.

Santorini has proven to be one of the most dramatic locations in the competition's calendar, with the eighteen finalists competing across the beautiful streets and alleyways of Oia.

For details of the 2018 competition released by Red Bull, please check our website in September.

Spa and fitness

There are a number of the larger hotels on the island that offer spa and gym facilities to non-residents. Three of the main resort spa centres are the Santorini Premium Spa, situated in the Museum Spa Wellness Hotel in Oia, the Venus Spa in Kamari and the Yolanda Liva in Perissa. However, most of the spas on the island offer a wide range of beauty therapies, whirlpool sessions and massages, for both male and female clients. I would advise you phone to enquire on the services that are available, the cost and availability especially in the high season.

Santorini Premium Spa: 22860 71055
Venus Spa: 22860 32760
Yolanda Liva: (*mobile*) 6949153369

Sub-aqua

There are three certified dive-centres on Santorini, namely the Volcano Diving Centre at Kamari beach, the Mediterranean Dive Club at Perissa and the Santorini Dive Centre, also at Perissa.

Water Park

Santorini Water Park as Perissa, has water-slides, three swimming pools with sunbeds and umbrellas, children's pools and other entertainments and amenities. It also has a relaxation area with pool bars and a restaurant. The park is open from 10:00 until midnight. However the water activities close at 19:00.

Admission is 6€, children half-price.

Getting around

For those who want the convenience, hiring a car is easy on Santorini. However, great care is needed as most of the roads twist and turn with many blind corners and precipitous drops with no safety barriers. If you are on the island for more than one week, it may be worth hiring a car for only some of your stay as the local bus service is reliable, air-conditioned and regular in the high season (*I have included bus information in a later chapter*).

Obviously this mode of transport is dependent on where you are staying and how accessible your hotel/apartment is to the local bus services. Most of the supermarkets on the bus routes sell tickets and will confirm the bus times.

Taxis are plentiful and taxi-drivers are expected to speak English, but the rule sometimes doesn't seem to be followed stringently.

The main taxi stand is just below Fira square, next to the old bus depot (*now used for parking bikes and mopeds*). Minimum charges start at 2€ and then it depends on where you go, if you share a taxi, the driver will consider each separate party as a second tariff. The time of day, the amount of luggage and if they have to pick you up, will all be taken into account in the final charge.

The **latest taxi charges** can be found on our website on the 'Santorini Travel Info' page. However, to give you some idea of cost, the fare from Fira to the airport will be around 12€ p.p, as will a journey from Fira to Oia.

Insider tip: It is always advisable to establish the fare before you get into the taxi.

Car Hire

If you decide to hire a car and you are travelling with a tour company, I am sure they will offer to arrange a hire car for you. Alternatively, there is a myriad of small car hire companies on the island and my experience is that they are all of high quality and open to negotiation, especially at the beginning and end of the season. In Fira town you will find the majority of companies on 25th

Martiou (*see page 170*), the road that leads up the hill north from the main square.

You can budget on paying around 250€ for one week's hire of, for example, a Daewoo Matiz or equivalent, which includes air conditioning which is a must especially in the high season and power steering, with prices increasing to around 370€ for the top end specification of a jeep. However, take account of the fact that although a jeep is seen as more of a fun vehicle and will go where the lower slung 2WD cars won't, it is open to the sun which is nice at first, but you can return home looking like a beetroot. On most models there is also nowhere to lock up your valuables.

I am not being condescending, but remember to bring your driving licence with you, an obvious thing you may say, but you would be surprised how often people forget and can't hire a car! The minimum age for hiring a car is between 21 and 23 years of age, dependent on the model of car and you need to have held the licence for at least a year. For non-EU residents, you are required by law to have an *International Driving Licence*.

Seat belts are compulsory and children under 10 are not allowed to travel in the front of the car. "Drinking and Driving" is a serious offence with harsh penalties, whether you are on two wheels or four. Police roadblocks for breath-tests, are a regular occurrence, especially in the summer months. Beware if you park illegally, the police will remove your registration plate and you will have to go and collect it from the police station, as well as of course, pay the appropriate fine. Also when travelling around the island, please be careful when parking in the villages, the roads are very narrow and the local buses weave their way through, with usually inches to spare between the bus and the houses. You will therefore be in trouble if you block the road.

I would also recommend that you take note of the advice of the car company as to which roads your particular vehicle is appropriate for. Many of the un-metalled interior roads look fine as you enter them, but they usually get progressively worse, with large potholes and sometimes with nowhere to turn around. If you don't hire a

4WD take care, or you may find yourself facing a hefty bill for any resulting damage to the car.

Fuel is readily available with modern service stations throughout the island. Prices per litre are around 1.50€ and that includes the personal service of an attendant filling the tank.

Roads are reasonably good between the resorts, but in the high season those in the towns can get very congested. One word of advice though, throughout the island there is a conspicuous lack of road signs, so make sure you obtain a copy of the hire companies road maps, or you may find yourself going round in circles.

Scooter, motorbike, quad bike and buggy hire

Now we come to the hire of scooters, motorbikes and quad bikes. Although initially very attractive, especially to the younger visitor (*as the cost is low and there are many hire companies promoting them*), I have seen so many serious accidents involving this type of transport in Greece. Therefore I would recommend anyone young or old, to think again and indulge themselves in the extra cost of a car. Although all the hire companies supply crash helmets, most people you see on two wheels (*or four in the case of a quad bike*), are dressed in shorts and T-shirts and I have seen the result of flesh contacting tarmac. Even at low speeds, the resulting injuries are enough to put anyone off the idea for life!

Many young tourists now see quad bikes as an exciting alternative to car or scooter hire, buy please note that most travel insurance companies now class quad bikes as a "dangerous sport" and do not cover their use. One unfortunate UK tourist to the island in 2011 was injured on a quad and had to be repatriated. The insurers dismissed his claim and he was left with a bill for £14,000!

If it's a more exciting mode of transport than a car that you desire and price is not a crucial consideration, then most motorbike rental shops offer four-wheel quad bikes for hire. The daily hire charge is around 50€.

However, I believe a safer alternative to a quad is the 'new kid on the block', a buggy.

Compared to quads they are much safer as their centre of gravity is lower and most models have a roll bar and safety belts as well as other extra features. Many hire companies are now offering this alternative to the quad, at a similar, if not the same price.

With regard to pedal cycles, I have noticed a surprising number of visitors using this form of transport, although there are a lot of hills on Santorini. For those who do enjoy cycling, I have included information on cycle hire in the chapter on *Sports and recreation*.

Finally, be careful whichever mode of transport you decide on, as the Highway Code is not stringently followed, especially at cross roads and with regard to "the right of way".

Bus information

Bus information

Travelling by bus within Santorini is not without its idiosyncrasies. Although there are routes to most of the main villages and beaches, bus timetables and frequencies change regularly and without notice. Also be aware that many of the public buses look like tour buses, so be careful not to make the mistake and miss your bus! The main KTEL bus depot is near the central square of Fira on the lower side road.

The latest bus timetable is available on our website on the 'Santorini Travel Info' page. Click the link and once on the KTEL website, click the flashing 'Timetable' in the top right of the page. However, to give you some basic information, I have added the following:

Winter season frequency   : every 1 - 1.5 hrs

Mid season frequency   : every hour to most areas

Summer season frequency   : every 30 minutes to most areas

The cost for all routes is between 1 and 2.50€.

The link between Athinios port and Fira bus depot are timed to get you to your ship between 1 and 1.5 hrs prior to its departure.

Bus routes

The bus to Oia goes via Firostefani and Imerovigli

The bus to Perissa goes via Karterados, Messaria, Pyrgos, Emborio, Megalochori and Perivolos.

The bus to Kamari goes via Karterados and Messaria

The bus to Vlychada goes via Karterados, Messaria, Pyrgos, Emborio, Megalochori and Perivolos.

The bus to Vourvoulos goes via Kontochori

The airport bus goes via Karterados, Messaria and Monolithos

The bus to Akrotiri goes via Karterados, Messaria and Vothonas

Early evening is one of the busiest times on the buses as the tourists head back to their accommodation from the beaches and villages. Very soon after starting you will find that there is only standing room left on the bus, so my advice is, return a little early to miss the rush.

There are no direct buses that go from one side of the island to the other. As Fira is the main bus depot, all routes both depart and arrive there. You therefore have to travel to the town and change buses for your onward journey to other villages, or beaches.

In the middle of the high season one can find Express buses that go to Perissa & Perivolos. The up side is they skip out some of the villages and you arrive quicker. The down side is that Express buses are often cancelled although advertised.

In the high season, some bus routes operate as late as 03:00, but check first. Bus tel.: 22860 25404 & 22860 23821

Food and drink are not allowed to be consumed on-board the buses and you should wear a top when travelling. This is to prevent sweat and suntan oil soiling the seats.

Road Train

A new 'road train' service, based in Fira, commenced operating three distinct tourist routes in late 2014. These include a guided tour of ancient Thera, a service linking Perissa and Glikada and finally from Oia to the local beaches of Baxedes to Kolumbo.

The cost of tickets range from 6€ to 25€ for the guided tour of Thera. However, at the time of going to press, it was not clear whether the tour of ancient Thera will run in 2018.

The 'road train' operates from 07:30 until late evening.

Ferry and hydrofoil information

Ferries to Santorini

The main Greek ferry route is from the port of Piraeus and dependent on the particular route, can stop at some the following islands before arriving at Santorini:- Paros, Naxos, Sikinos, Folegranros, Anafi, Kithnos, Milos, Kimolos and Ios. High-speed ferries and hydrofoils destined for Santorini, mostly use the port of Rafina. In summer there are daily services from both these ports.

A normal ferry takes around nine hours to reach the port of Santorini from Piraeus, with the modern *Blue Star Ferries* taking around seven hours. Hydrofoils complete the journey in around four to five hours.

The port of Rafina is located one hour from the centre of Athens and is the nearest port to the International Airport of A.Venizelos.

Contact telephone numbers:

Port authority   : 22860 22239
Ferry company   : 22860 22202

Santorini to the other islands of the Aegean

Santorini has ferry connections with most of the Cyclades islands, such as Mykonos, Anafi, Amorgos, Naxos, Paros, Ios, Rhodes and Crete.

The island is also linked with the rest of the islands of the Dodecanese and with Mykonos, Syros, Samos and Thessaloniki.

Daily hydrofoils also serve the islands of Samos, Ikaria and Fourni in the north-eastern Aegean.

If you are spending more than a week on Santorini, I would recommend taking a ferry or hydrofoil to one of the nearby islands. Local travel agents will be able to confirm timetables, what is available on the islands and what to take with you. But be careful not to miss the last boat back!

Comprehensive information on ferries can be found on the 'Santorini Travel Information' page on the website.

Excursion boats

From the port below Fira, there are a wide range of excursions and private boat hire available. From trips around the island's coast, a visit to the volcano (*see page 81*), private yacht hire to the other islands in the Cyclades, on-board wedding receptions, conferences and many more.

You can also take a ferry from the ports at Amoudi or Athinios to Thirasia, the second largest island in the archipelago However, there are no sandy beaches on the island and little to recommend other than peace and solitude and some beautiful views.

Details of these can be obtained from the companies in the port or through the many travel agents in Fira and the other resorts.

Distances on the island (*in km*)

	FIRA	IA (OIA)	KAMARI	IMEROVIGLI	FIROSTEFANI	PERISSA	MESSARIA	PERIVOLOS	AGIOS GEORGIOS	PIRGOS	VLYCHADA	EMPORIO	MEGALOCHORI	EXO GONIA	AKROTIRI	KARTERADOS	VOURVOULOS	MONOLITHOS	AIRPORT	PORT ATHINIOS
FIRA		9.42	7.37	2.24	0.92	11.23	3.03	10.93	10.51	4.74	10.35	8.28	5.24	5.56	9.37	2.02	2.69	7.11	5.33	7.63
IA (OIA)	9.42		16.79	7.18	8.50	20.65	12.45	20.35	19.93	14.16	19.77	17.70	14.66	14.98	18.79	11.44	6.73	16.53	14.75	17.05
KAMARI	7.37	16.79		9.61	8.29	11.48	4.34	11.29	10.91	4.86	11.88	9.01	6.94	2.36	11.09	5.80	9.73	7.06	5.48	9.27
IMEROVIGLI	2.24	7.18	9.61		1.32	13.47	5.27	13.17	12.75	6.98	12.59	10.52	7.48	7.80	11.61	2.94	0.45	9.35	7.57	9.87
FIROSTEFANI	0.92	8.50	8.29	1.32		12.15	3.95	11.85	11.43	5.66	11.27	9.20	6.16	6.48	12.53	2.94	1.77	8.03	6.25	8.55
PERISSA	11.23	20.65	11.48	13.47	12.15		9.97	1.16	2.85	8.74	5.30	2.98	6.19	9.71	7.40	11.11	13.92	13.38	12.18	10.57
MESSARIA	3.03	12.45	4.34	5.27	3.95	9.97		9.67	9.14	3.04	8.72	6.83	3.76	2.25	7.91	1.49	5.72	3.91	2.10	6.46
PERIVOLOS	10.93	20.35	11.29	13.17	11.85	1.16	9.67		1.68	8.47	3.80	2.53	5.76	9.25	7.10	10.62	13.62	13.08	11.87	10.27
AGIOS GEORGIOS	10.51	19.93	10.91	12.75	11.43	2.85	9.14	1.68		8.07	2.55	2.24	5.39	8.78	6.52	10.23	13.20	12.58	11.44	9.85
PIRGOS	4.74	14.16	4.86	6.98	5.66	8.74	3.04	8.47	8.07		7.78	6.08	2.75	2.64	6.36	4.77	7.93	6.62	5.15	5.20
VLYCHADA	10.35	19.77	11.88	12.59	11.27	5.30	8.72	3.80	2.55	7.78		3.40	5.15	8.78	5.45	9.98	13.04	12.72	11.28	9.62
EMPORIO	8.28	17.70	9.01	10.52	9.20	2.98	6.83	2.53	2.24	6.08	3.40		3.23	6.73	4.44	8.09	10.97	10.75	9.19	7.64
MEGALOCHORI	5.24	14.66	6.94	7.48	6.16	6.19	3.76	5.76	5.39	2.75	5.15	3.23		4.64	4.15	5.01	7.93	7.68	6.21	4.37
EXO GONIA	5.56	14.98	2.36	7.80	6.48	9.71	2.25	9.25	8.78	2.64	8.78	6.73	4.64		8.67	3.82	8.25	5.22	3.67	7.09
AKROTIRI	9.37	18.79	11.09	11.61	12.53	7.40	7.91	7.10	6.52	6.36	5.45	4.44	4.15	8.67		9.09	12.06	11.83	10.37	8.49
KARTERADOS	2.02	11.44	5.80	2.94	2.94	11.11	1.49	10.62	10.23	4.77	9.98	8.09	5.01	3.82	9.09		3.82	5.41	3.71	7.46
VOURVOULOS	2.69	6.73	9.73	0.45	1.77	13.92	5.72	13.62	13.20	7.93	13.04	10.97	7.93	8.25	12.06	3.82		9.75	7.86	8.02
MONOLITHOS	7.11	16.53	7.06	9.35	8.03	13.38	3.91	13.08	12.58	6.62	12.72	10.75	7.68	5.22	11.83	5.41	9.75		2.58	10.28
AIRPORT	5.33	14.75	5.48	7.57	6.25	12.18	2.10	11.87	11.44	5.15	11.28	9.19	6.21	3.67	10.37	3.71	7.86	2.58		8.65
PORT ATHINIOS	7.63	17.05	9.27	9.87	8.55	10.57	6.46	10.27	9.85	5.20	9.62	7.64	4.37	7.09	8.49	7.46	8.02	10.28	8.65	

Courtesy of www.santorini.gr

Eating and drinking

In this chapter I will first cover dining out. During the writing of this book I have meticulously sought to be unbiased and accurate with all the information I have included. However, where dining out is concerned, we have all had the disappointing experience of a poor meal in a highly recommended restaurant. Both differing tastes and changing circumstances can mean that a good restaurant to one person can be unacceptable to another. Also, as most restaurants on the island are seasonal, staff tend to move from one establishment to another, year to year and even during the season, which can affect the quality. Therefore in this chapter, I believe it is wise not to recommend any particular restaurants or tavernas on the island, but instead try to outline some basic information and useful hints.

I will say, that I have rarely had a poor meal on the island, but on that odd occasion, I have found it hard to complain when the average price of an evening meal is around 30€ per person including a glass of wine.

The tips I would pass on are as follows:

First take a good look at the taverna or restaurant in question, is it busy, does it have pleasant surroundings? A major part of dining out on holiday is I believe the service, surroundings and views. Remember though, on Santorini you pay for the views, all the prices are higher in those restaurants and bars that perch on the caldera rim. Before deciding look at the menu, is it comprehensive? Don't be put off by the faded photographs of food outside the restaurant or taverna, most are like this and if you were to stand outside in the sun all day you would fade too! If you fancy fish, ask if it is fresh, by law they have to specify this. A further tip, especially outside the main resorts, look to see if the locals are eating in the restaurant, they know where to find the best food!

Service in most of the restaurants is good, if sometimes a little slow, especially when it comes to obtaining the bill, but remember you are on holiday, so relax. It is acceptable for you to ask to look at the food in the kitchen and enquire about any particular dish. You may feel a little wary at doing so, but whenever I have asked, they have been more than happy to show me around and answer any questions.

Most dishes come with French fries and/or rice and often with a small amount of salad. If you are partial to salad, it may be advisable to order an extra portion, but as you will find, they are usually large, so one should be enough for two people.

If, after your main course you do not order a pudding, many tavernas will bring some melon, mousse, or honey cake on the house to thank you for your custom, or you will get a small glass of Ouzo or Metaxa with the bill. It is worth keeping an eye out to see what that particular taverna's approach is. One further point to remember is that in Greece the salt and pepper pots tend to be the opposite way round, i.e. the salt pot has multiple holes and the pepper a single hole.

Most tavernas and restaurants are open all day serving breakfast, lunch and dinner. For those who want a more British start to the day a well-cooked and comprehensive English breakfast can be obtained at some tavernas, with only the bacon being a little different, but still very tasty. The cost with juice, tea or coffee, the usual egg, bacon, sausage, beans, tomatoes and toast is between 8 and 12€. The alternative of a continental breakfast is always available. Lunch, if you can manage it after breakfast, is invariably the same menu as used in the evenings, but most places do snacks and salads as an alternative.

If during your visit you want something a little different from traditional Greek cuisine, there is a Chinese and a Mexican restaurant on the island. China restaurant is near the cable car in Fira and the Mexican restaurant, Señor Zorba, is about 3km south of Fira on the road to Megalochori.

In the towns and larger villages, there are a number of fast food outlets such as the Toast Club in Fira, where you can eat in, or buy a take away such as a rotisserie chicken, kebab, or burger meal.

(A list of independently reviewed quality restaurants can be found on the 'Santorini Links' page on our website).

A quick guide to Greek food

For those less familiar with Greek food, on the following pages I have outlined the main dishes you will find in the majority of tavernas *(in alphabetical order)*.

Appetisers

Dolmades - Vine leaves stuffed with rice and then rolled, a hot variation can also contains minced meat. Served most often cold as an appetiser, but can also be served hot with an avgolemono sauce on top. Its origin is thought to be from Thebes about the time of Alexander the Great.

Keftedes - Small rissoles or fritters often made with minced lamb, pork or veal, onion, egg and herbs and sometimes with ouzo as a moistener. Keftedes are shaped into flattened balls and usually fried. On Santorini, one local speciality is their *Tomato Keftedes*.

Mezes - A plate containing a selection of different appetisers, similar to the Spanish tapas, usually to be shared around the table. Mezes can include seafood, meats, vegetable dishes and dips.

Taramosalata - Greek caviar combined with breadcrumbs, oil, onion, and lemon juice to compliment any meal as an appetiser. This is a thick pink or white puree of fish roe, dependent on the type of fish. Sometimes mashed potato is substituted for breadcrumbs.

Tzatziki - A yoghurt, cucumber and garlic dip to be served chilled on its own, or with pita or plain bread and great on a Gyro.

The following three appetisers are traditional Santorinian dishes:-

Fava - Yellow Santorinian lentils

Tomato Balls

White Eggplant dip

Main courses

Grilled meats - Grilled meat usually includes lamb chops, pork, veal and chicken, either plain or in a variety of sauces dependent on the restaurant.

Gyro - Thin slices of barbecued meat specially seasoned with herbs and spices, served with tomatoes and onions on pita bread, and topped with tzatziki. Best from a rotisserie.

Kleftico or Klephtiko - Is a term that refers to any kind of meat dish that is sealed and baked. The word comes from the time of the Greek revolution, when bands of Greek guerrillas, called Klephts, hid in the mountains and cooked their dinner in pits sealed with mud, so that smoke and steam would not escape and betray their position. Usually it will be Lamb Kleftico that is on the menu.

Moussaka - A Greek national dish, Moussaka is prepared with sliced eggplant, lean ground beef, onions, tomatoes, butter, eggs, milk, cheese and seasonings and baked in an oven.

Omelette - Most tavernas offer a variety of omelettes on their menu.

Pasta - Spaghetti Bolognese is a firm favourite on most menus and they usually do it very well, but a wide range of other pasta dishes are normally available.

Pastitsio - A Greek Lasagne combining macaroni, minced meat, cheese and covered with béchamel sauce.

Pilafi - Fluffy rice simmered in butter, spices and rich chicken stock.

Pizza - Where pizzas are concerned there are some tavernas that specialise, having the proper ovens and expertise. So my advice would be to ask around to find the best place to go, but personally I have found most are at least equivalent in quality to the best in the UK or US.

Roast Chicken - Both from an oven or a spit, cooked in olive oil. I personally think the rotisserie chickens are the best and taste as chicken should taste. Chicken in most restaurants on the island tends to be in fillet form, although, there are a few tavernas where you can still get a half chicken on the bone.

Roast Lamb - Lamb prepared in the traditional Greek way, roasted with herbs and olive oil.

Seafood - As with the majority of Mediterranean countries, in Greece you can find a wide variety of fresh and tasty seafood. Before ordering though, I suggest you ask if the fish is fresh and not frozen. Many restaurants and tavernas have a chilled fresh seafood cabinet near the entrance and the waiters are usually happy to confirm the choice of fresh fish they have on offer.

Souvlaki - Souvlaki are made from cubes of meat that have been marinated for several hours in olive oil, lemon juice & origano, then threaded on wooden skewers and grilled or barbequed. They can be beef, veal, chicken, lamb or pork.

Spanakopitta - Spanakopitta is a spinach pie, about the size of a flan. These small pies are made with a spinach and feta cheese filling in filo pastry. In Greek bakeries they are referred to as Spanakopittes, but don't be confused they can also be called Spanakotiropitakia.

Stamnato - Usually made with lamb (*or spelt lamp or lab!*) with potatoes in tomato and garlic sauce, baked in a traditional pot called a Lamm.

Stifado - Stifado is a casserole made of beef, veal or lamb in wine with pearl onions, tomatoes, herbs and spices.

If you fancy splashing out on a lobster dinner, those restaurants that have fresh lobster on their menu usually require 24 hrs notice; I would also ask what the price would be per person and not per kilo. If you order prawns, the average price, away from the caldera edge, is around 12€ and you get about six king-sized in their shell.

Patisseries

Baklava - Nut filled, paper-thin layers of glazed filo pastry soaked in pure honey make this the king of pastry desserts. Every country in the near-east claims baklava is its own.

Diples - Honey rolls so thin and flaky that they crumble when they are bitten.

Halva - Is a candy made from ground sesame seeds. It is an oriental originated sweet, popular in Greece.

Loukoumades - Feathery light honey tokens or sweet fritters, deep fried to a golden brown and dipped in boiling honey. A tasty delight from ancient Greece, when they were given as prizes to winners of athletic games.

Kataifi - A delicious pastry made of shredded filo pastry rolled with nuts and honey and sprinkled with syrup. Found throughout the Mediterranean.

Koulouria - Also called Koulourakia - Breaded butter cookies with a light sugar glaze, perfect with coffee.

Kourabiedes - Sugar covered crescent shaped cakes that melt in your mouth. They are usually served at weddings, at Christmas, and on special occasions, such as birthdays and holidays.

Melomakarona - A honey cookie sprinkled with a spice-nut mixture.

Coffee

Greek style coffee - This is a thick, powdered coffee that is made in a brickee (*or brika*), which is traditionally a small brass pot with a long handle. Modern advances have given us stainless steel brikas. This is not instant coffee, and even though powdered, the coffee used does not dissolve. The grounds settle to the bottom of the cup.

When you order coffee of any sort, you must specify plain, sweet or medium-sweet (*sketo, glyko or metrio in Greek, respectively*). You can also order Cappuccino, Expresso and other types of coffee in most restaurants. Tea is usually available, but it comes in a do-it yourself style and can taste a little odd due to the long-life milk often used. I would recommend you ask for fresh milk.

Ouzeries

A traditional Greek style of eating out is at an Ouzerie, a blend of bar and taverna. Ouzeries usually only offer mezedes and possibly a few seasonal dishes, with (*if you want to be really Greek*) an Ouzo, Souma, or Retsina as an accompanying drink. Mezedes comprise a selection of small dishes or appetizers, placed on a platter or around the table for you to pick and choose.

Insider tip: This is recommended as an easy and cost effective way to sample some traditional Greek food.

Supermarkets

The supermarkets in Fira and the villages are well provisioned for the international holidaymaker. Many brands are recognisable and if not, the supermarket staff are usually very helpful. Milk comes in cartons printed with the Greek word 'γαλα' (*pronounced yarla*), the required percentage and whether skimmed or semi-skimmed. As is the case in the US, what the English know as crisps are called chips in Greece and chips are known as French fries. Supermarket and tavern staff are though familiar with both terminologies.

If you want to eat in, supermarkets usually have a wide selection of fresh vegetables and fruit on sale, but meat, other than the basics such as cooked cold meats and bacon have to be bought from the local butcher, just ask and they will tell you where it is.

There are takeaways in the main resorts with a good choice of fast-food, alternatively if you don't have the facilities to cook meat in your accommodation, many tavernas and restaurants will do a take-away service for main meat items such as a roast chicken.

If you want bread or pastries for later on in the day, I would advise you buy them early, as the supermarkets tend to sell out before lunchtime.

All the supermarkets sell wines and spirits, with most of the international brands of spirits being readily available on the island. The selection of lagers is also international, although most are brewed in Greece. The Greek lagers, such as Mythos and Vergina are in my view good, but if you are looking for a more Western-European style lager, try Kaiser. In addition to the supermarkets, there are usually dedicated off-licences in the main resorts that stock an even greater range. Prices are at least comparable with the UK and US, if not cheaper.

Shopping

Cigarettes, sweets and newspapers

In all the towns and resorts you will notice large wooden kiosks on the pavements of the main streets. This is where in Greece you traditionally buy such items as cigarettes and tobacco, newspapers, magazines, ice-cream, drinks, sweets and snacks such as crisps. The supermarkets also sell all of these except usually newspapers.

If you smoke and are visiting from an EU country, don't bother bringing any with you as they cheaper than back home, at approximately 4€ for a packet of 20. You needn't shop around as the price will be the same at all the outlets. All the main international brands are available such as Marlboro, Rothmans, Superkings, Benson & Hedges, etc.

As Greece is in the EU, the rule banning smoking in any enclosed building also applies here. In summer though, most tavernas and bars are open-air, so you are free to indulge.

For those who become homesick whilst away and want to know what new stealth taxes the government have imposed, English newspapers are available, although they may be the previous day's edition. I have personally seen on sale from the UK (*although printed in Greece*) The Daily Mail, The Mirror, The Sun and a couple of the main broadsheets, so you should have a good choice.

Links to the websites of all the major UK and US newspapers and live TV news bulletins can be found on our website in the 'Santorini News' section.

Magazines in English are rarer, but I have seen some of the main women's publications on the newsstands.

Men's clothes

Santorini is unlike other Greek islands in that it receives a considerable number of cruise-liner visitors. Due to this prices are a little higher than elsewhere in Greece, especially in Fira. However, what you will find is that there is an excellent choice and the quality tends to be high. There is a good selection of linen and cotton shirts with prices starting at around 30€, with T-shirts, light weight trousers, shorts, summer jackets, hats and belts making up the majority of goods on offer. The variety and range for females tends to be greater, but then most men don't go on holiday to shop!

Personal electronic items

I have yet to survey in detail the cost of personal electronic equipment, but for the UK tourist, my initial view is that the prices are equivalent to those back home and as Greece is in the European Union, there will be no duty to pay on your return.

However, it may be a problem if the goods turn out to be faulty. If you do intend to purchase expensive items, check first that the manufacturer's guarantee will cover the item back in your country of residence.

Souvenirs

Well this is a difficult subject to write about as we all have a different view of what a good souvenir is. In all the resorts, but especially in Fira, the shops are designer in nature and in many the prices reflect this. Jewellery, art and glassware shops abound, so much so you wonder how each can make a living. If you browse their windows you will see most of the fashionable and exclusive makers names from around the world. There *are* shops selling the less expensive souvenir items and I have to say the quality is generally high. You will also find many unusual souvenir items made from the volcanic rock of the island, but if you really get stuck, there is always the bottle of Ouzo, Metaxa or a natural bath sponge.

With regard to cosmetics, fashion, hairdressers and jewellery, I will pass this section over to my partner Carol.

Cosmetics

Although Santorini is an island, as far as buying your moisturiser, body lotions, make-up etc and the all-important sunscreen you don't have to worry. Especially in the towns there is a good selection of retailers that stock most cosmetics and toiletries.
There are specialised beauty shops in Fira and most pharmacies and supermarkets sell known international products. If you cannot find your favourite brand then just ask an assistant who will be able to advise you on the Greek equivalent product. So no need to waste valuable space and weight in your suitcase, just buy all you need when you arrive.

Fashion

Thira has an extensive array of different shops to cater for every taste and age group, from fun boutiques, to designer outlets. In Fira it is best to shop around first though, as depending on where the shop is situated depends on the price! Shops on the cable car route and near the caldera edge tend to be more expensive, where as if you deviate down the side alleys you will find the same items at a cheaper price, with no compromise on quality.

There is such a wide choice, from bikinis and sarongs, to leather shoes and handbags you will be spoilt for choice!

Hairdressers

There are salons in Fira and in most of the main resorts to cater for all your follicle needs, and after a few days in the sun and sea, what better way to treat your hair, and yourself, than having a few hours relaxation and pampering, preparing for your evening out in one of the many restaurants and tavarnas.

Jewellery

It seems that nearly every other shop you pass in Fira and the larger resorts sell some kind of jewellery, bangles, bracelets, rings, necklaces, earrings and much more. Designer and specialised jewellery shops are in abundance in Fira where some retailers design and manufacture their own ranges. I especially like the designs made from the local black lava stone, very different and unique, and something to treasure and keep as a memory of your visit to this beautiful island.

U.K. Customs

Regarding taking goods back home, if the goods you are carrying have had tax paid in Greece you do not have to pay any tax or duty on them in the UK. Any alcohol or tobacco you bring in must be for your own use and transported by you.

Own use includes goods for your own consumption and gifts. If you bring in goods for resale, or for any payment, even payment in kind, they are regarded as being for a commercial purpose.

With regards to quantities allowed, you are particularly likely to be asked questions by customs officers if you have more than:

800 cigarettes, 200 cigars, 400 cigarillos, 1 kg tobacco, 110 litres of beer, 90 litres of wine, 10 litres of spirits, 20 litres of fortified wine such as port or sherry.

Some goods are banned, such as plant materials that could contain diseases.

The information above is correct at the time of going to press.

Money matters

Most of the banks are located around Fira's main square and the road leading from Fira to the port of Athinios, but there is a branch of the National Bank in Kamari and braches of Alpha Bank and Eurobank in Oia. All the banks have ATM machines (*hole in the wall*), which take most debit and credit cards.*

The charges for the use of your card will for the most part depend on your bank back home, so it might be wise to have a discussion with your bank/building society before you leave home and confirm the costs you will incur. If you use one of the banks on the island to exchange your US or UK currency or traveller's cheques take your passport with you to confirm your identity.

Other than the banks, there are a broad choice of exchange options, many hotels, shops and car hire companies will also exchange Sterling and US Dollars, but make sure you check the rate and any charges first. Again the Greeks are very honest and I have never been short-changed, but it is best to check.

In the banks, you may find a queue and remember life is at a slow pace in Greece. Look around as there may be a ticket-machine where you are required to take a numbered ticket identifying your place in the queue.

As to the exchange rate, I certainly have found that it is generally equal or better than that found back in the UK, so if you don't want the hassle of picking up currency before you leave home, just bring cash and change it on the island, for an example in July 2017 the exchange rate in the UK was 1.14 on the island it was 1.16.

Credit/Debit cards are accepted in many tavernas and shops on the island. Just in case though, it is advisable to carry sufficient money with you on days and evenings out. One further point regarding drawing cash out abroad via a credit card (*learnt from personal experience*), is that many card companies will not only charge you a relatively high exchange commission, but also an additional cash advance fee. So if you want to use your credit card abroad, I would therefore advise you check on potential charges before leaving home.

With regard to the safety of carrying money and leaving it in your room, as I have stressed before, the Greeks are extremely honest and over the last 30 years of travelling in Greece, I have never had anything stolen. On the contrary, I have accidentally left valuable items in public places, only to find them untouched hours later. Remember though, there are not only Greeks on the island!

At the time of going to press, the main currencies were unstable and therefore, I have not included rates here. However, the latest exchange rates and both Visa and MasterCard ATM locators* can be found on our website. At the top of the homepage click the 'Travel Club' tab, then 'Travel Club Santorini' and finally 'Santorini Travel Info'.

The bank opening hours are Monday to Thursday: 08:00 - 14:30, Friday: 08:00 - 14:00.

Insider tip: *If you are exchanging money, it is advisable to be at the bank well before 14:00.*

Bank phone numbers

National Bank of Greece (*Fira*) : 22860 22662

    "   "   "   " (*Kamari*) : 22860 34133

Emporiki Bank (*Fira*) : 22860 22534

Alpha Bank (*Fira*) : 22860 23801

    "   " (*Oia*) : 22860 71867

Agricultural Bank : 22860 22738

Pireus : 22860 25441

Eurobank (*Fira*) : 22860 25739

    " (*Oia*) : 22860 71342

Weather

What can you say about the weather in Greece other than it is invariably fabulous. To be more precise, what we would call summer back in the UK usually starts in May with temperatures rising throughout the following months (*see the table below*). Through late April, May and early June, and then again in October, the weather can be compared to a good British summer.

The months of July and August tend to be the hottest, with average daily temperatures ranging from 82°F (*28°C*) during the day to 72°F (*22°C*) at night. The high temperatures often spark off thunderstorms in the evening, but these are not usually accompanied by rain and are more entertaining than a nuisance.

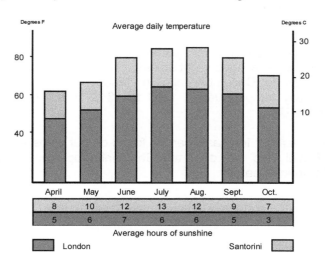

	April	May	June	July	Aug.	Sept.	Oct.
	8	10	12	13	12	9	7
	5	6	7	6	6	5	3

Average hours of sunshine

London ■   Santorini ▢

Rainfall is almost non-existent in summer, but showers can be expected between October and March.

In late April and May, the island often experiences strong breezes, but this can be of benefit, especially when the hot summer sun arrives early.

The Meltemi

The Meltemi (*the Greek equivalent of the French Mistral*) is a powerful wind that blows across all of the Aegean islands. It is the result of a high-pressure system over the Balkans and a low-pressure system over Turkey, creating strong northeast winds. The Meltemi occurs mainly during the summer with July and August being the worst affected months, but it can spring up occasionally in May and October. It usually starts in the early afternoon and can die out at sunset although occasionally, it will last through the night and repeat for three to six, sometimes even ten days. The winds can cause havoc with the ferry timetables and remember not to leave valuables on your balcony, or you may return to find them missing!

In October the evenings begin to cool, but that can be a blessing for those who enjoy a good night's sleep. Temperatures continue to drop through to December and in January and February the average daily temperature is 10°C to 13°C, which is more like spring in the UK.

The latest weather forecasts can be found on our website by going to the 'Travel Club' tab, open the 'Santorini' drop-down menu and go to 'Santorini Weather'.

Bugs, biters and things

Bugs, bites and things

This chapter is not for the paranoid, as I have been true to my word adding a definitive list of the bugs and biters on the island. However, that does not mean that any of the following are a threat to life and limb and I can confirm that regarding all listed, I have never met anyone who has suffered more than the usual mosquito bites or the very rare wasp sting, so with that in mind, the facts are:-

Bees

Bees are less likely to sting than wasps, the reason being that the unlike the wasp the bee stinger has barbs which prevents the insect withdrawing it. Brushing the bee off, therefore results in the stinger and venom sack being ripped out of the insect, inevitably this leads to its death.

Stingers should be scraped out sideways with a credit card, finger nail, or any sharp object. This helps to prevent squeezing the venom sack, which would lead to further venom being injected.

Treatment of the sting:-

1. Pull stinger out.
2. Cool compresses with ice.
3. Diphenhydramne (*Benadryl*) should be given to decrease minimal allergic reactions.
4. If a severe allergic reaction occurs, seek medical advice immediately.

Creams can be obtained from pharmacies to reduce the itching and inflammation.

Centipedes

Centipedes are not usually found in urban areas, they prefer rural and forested areas. Centipedes can bite humans, millipedes don't. The centipede's venom causes pain and swelling in the area of the bite, and may cause other reactions throughout the body.

The majority of bites are not life-threatening to humans and present the greatest risk to children and those who develop allergic reactions. If bitten, consult a doctor or pharmacist at the earliest opportunity.

Hornets

There are hornets on Santorini, but small numbers mean they are not a problem. They have a fearsome reputation for stinging and causing considerable harm, but in fact their stings are only a little more painful than that of a wasp or bee, due to the fact that hornet venom contains a larger amount (5%) of acetylcholine. Like most bees and wasps they usually only sting if you are blocking a flight path or are moving rapidly; however, nests should be avoided at all costs as a swarm attack can be very serious! For those that are not familiar with hornets, they have similar colouring to a wasp, being a member of the wasp family, but are about twice the size.

Horse Flies

Found throughout warmer climates, the Horse Fly is the largest of the fly species. Recognised by its size and a grey mottling on the back of the thorax, only the female fly bites prior to egg-laying. If you do get bitten, make sure the fly is either swatted or gone, as they can be persistent little critters, drinking blood from the wound.

Treat any wound as you would a mosquito bite.

Jellyfish stings

If you do experience a sting, the quickest remedy is to apply urine to the affected area, so pick your holiday companions carefully!

Lizards

You will see many wall lizards whilst on Santorini, most abundantly on the hillside of Mesa Vouno. The most common species is Erhard's Wall Lizards, but don't worry they are totally harmless.

Mosquitoes

As with the whole of the Mediterranean there are mosquitoes on the island, but they only appear in significant numbers in July and August, but a good covering of mosquito repellent in the evenings, which is sold at all supermarkets, should generally protect you. It does seem to be dependent on the person, I rarely get bitten, whereas my partner Carol seems to attract all the little critters. Her answer is she has better quality blood!

I would advise you to use a mosquito machine in your bedroom, which can be the old plug-in heated tablet type (*the tablets are still available*), or the new heated liquid system. After testing the latter, they are in my view superior, one bottle of liquid should last for the whole holiday and there are no fiddly tablets to change every day.

Mosquito bites

Although there are over the counter remedies available at the local pharmacies, you could try applying vinegar to the bites and you will find the itchiness will subside.

Scorpions

Rarely seen, the species found on Santorini is *Euscorpius Germanus*, also called the Small Wood-scorpion. As their common name implies, they are small at around 2 - 3cm in length and dark brown in colour. They tend to hide in crevices and such places as wood piles. In the most unlikely event that you are stung, the effect of the venom of this species is usually no worse than a wasp sting.

Sea Urchins

As is the case with beaches anywhere in the world, sea urchins can be found in some beach areas on the island. If you have children, a quick chat at one of the beach tavernas, or a scan for their remains on the beach will confirm whether to take precautions. If they are around the simplest solution is to wear swim shoes when entering the sea.

If you do step on one, consult a doctor or pharmacist and they will advise you on the best course of action. Don't worry though, it will usually mean nothing more serious than a little discomfort.

Here is the advice given in a medical journal:-

- Look for the signs and symptoms of a sea urchin sting: small spines embedded in the skin; a localized brownish-purple colour where the barbs made contact with the skin.
- Use sterile tweezers to remove any embedded spines.
- Control bleeding by applying direct pressure to the wound.
- Irrigate the wound with an irrigation syringe.
- Clean the wound with a disinfectant solution.
- Immerse the foot in hot water for at least 30 minutes, until pain subsides.
- Elevate the foot to control swelling.
- Dress the wound with a sterile bandage.
- Monitor for signs of infection. These signs include swelling, redness, pus, red lines radiating from the site of the wound, heat at the site of the wound, and fever.
- Seek medical advice.

Snakes

With regard to snakes, I have only seen one that was crossing the road and I saw it too late, it is now a flat-snake! There are a number of species on the island as in all of Greece, but only one is poisonous, namely the Viper. Most vipers are nocturnal and are only sporadically observed in the daylight, when they bask or mate. It is easy to distinguish a viper from the harmless species, based on their triangular head, swollen cheeks, stout body and a zig-zag pattern on their back (*vipers are seldom longer than one metre*). A viper bite is not necessarily poisonous: in only about 30% of bites there is actual injection of venom, and thus a need for anti-venom treatment.

The rule is if you see a snake, be on the safe-side and leave it well alone, but *please* be assured, it is extremely rare to hear of a bite. The main precautions that can be taken are that when out walking in long grass, wear ankle length boots and do not turn large stones over, or place your hand into crevices that might be home to a snake. If you were to be the one in a million and are bitten, the advice is to be safe and seek medical help straight away.

Wasps

A more irritating insect can be the wasp. They tend to be found in greater numbers near the populated beaches where there is a good supply of tourist food, with the areas around towns and villages having very few if any. So it is dependent on where you are and what you are doing. I can honestly say don't worry, the locals don't, just try to ignore them. In five years I haven't been stung and just find them irritating at times. Another answer is to buy a fly swat and see how many you can exterminate. Sorry, I apologise to the entomologists amongst you.

If you find them irritating when you eating in a restaurant, ask the waiter for a "burner", usually a metal container filled with smouldering Greek coffee. The fumes are surprisingly an excellent deterrent to the little blighters. The good news is that come sundown they all return to their nest.

If you are unfortunate enough to get stung, the cheapest and quickest solution is to simply apply vinegar to the affected area. However, if you are allergic to stings, seek medical advice as soon as possible.

Creams to reduce the inflammation and itching can be purchased from pharmacies.

Other insects

The other insects you may observe whilst on Santorini are a wide variety of moths and butterflies, praying mantis and bumble bees.

Health

Hospitals, doctors & community clinics

Whereas we all hope that nothing untoward happens on our holidays, especially health wise, as I can personally testify it sometimes does.

My view of the islands facilities is a good one, with all but the most serious incidents catered for on the island itself. In Fira there is a Health Centre, well equipped and easy to find by following the signs in the town.

There are also private doctors in Fira and most of the resorts. Normally the surgery is near the middle of the village or resort centre and can be recognised by a red cross on the door, or on a sign in front of the building.

There are a number of pharmacies in Fira and at least one in each of the resorts. They operate on regular business hours (*usually 08:00 - 13:00 and 18:00 - 24:00*). One pharmacy in Fira stays open during the night and the early morning hours, they work on a rota system so you need to check locally. You will find the quality of medicines and advice is equal to that back home.

For emergencies there is a twenty-four hour doctor service at the Health Centre in Fira. Alternatively there are private doctors you can visit if the need arises.

Remember, if you are an EU citizen, you should apply for a European Health Insurance Card (*EHIC*), designated the A1 card. This will allow you to obtain free or reduced cost treatment abroad; this includes only treatment provided on the state scheme. The EHIC is free of charge and in the UK can be obtained in the following ways. I advise that you apply well in advance of your trip, as it can take a week or two for the card to arrive:

By internet at **www.ehic.org.uk**
By telephone on 08456062030
Or by form from the Post Office

Dental services

My own personal experience of ill health in Greece was in 2006, prior to moving to the island of Thassos to live. Only hours after arriving on the island, I was stricken by severe toothache and although I suffered for two further days (*I'm a man*), in the end I had to ask for help and I was recommended to a dentist in Thassos Town.

All I can say is that I was amazed at the care shown to me on my arrival and the quality of the subsequent treatment. The surgery was modern, comfortable and very well equipped and the dentist friendly, he spoke fluent English and his chair-side manner was highly professional. I also found on my return to the UK, that the charges I had paid were less than half that I would have paid at home. All in all, I have to say that if I required dental work, I would prefer to have it done in Greece, rather than back in the UK.

Contact details:

Santorini Health Centre, Tel: 22863 60300-2

Emergency services, Tel: 112 (*Ambulance 166*)

Community clinics:

First aid phone numbers:

Fira	: 22860 22237
Emporio	: 22860 81222
Kamari	: 22860 31175
Oia	: 22860 71227
Pyrgos	: 22860 31207
Thirassia	: 22860 23191

Dentist

Fira Dentist	: 22860 23685

Stomach upset

If the worst happens, try adding a little fresh lemon juice to a Greek coffee and knock it back (*so you don't taste it*) and in no time at all the symptoms will ease.

Sunburn

The most obvious advice anyone can give is to be extra careful for at least the first few days! If like most, you are not used to the Mediterranean sun, take it very easy and use plenty of high factor sun-block cream. You are especially vulnerable when there is a breeze, or when you are travelling in an open top car, a point I learnt from bitter experience, as you do not feel the full extent of your skin's reaction to the sun.

If the worst does happen, my first advice is to visit the local pharmacy and seek help. If this is not possible, a cold shower will initially relieve the pain, but drip dry, as using a towel will only aggravate the situation. For mild sunburn, cool compresses with equal parts of milk and water may suffice. Another remedy, recommended by many, is to spray or pat the affected areas with white or cider vinegar; this will relieve the pain and itching and hopefully give you a good night's sleep until you can visit a pharmacy.

The symptoms may also be relieved by taking aspirin or ibuprofen, but do not exceed the doses specified on the label.

(Our website contains a comprehensive 'Holiday Advice' section, with help regarding health issues).

Safety

Where safety is concerned, the subject falls into two categories.

First there is the safety aspect with regard to crime; one of the points that has always attracted me to Greece, especially the islands, is the lack of both property and personal crime. It does exist, or there wouldn't be police or prisons in Greece, but as far as the tourist is concerned it is rare on Santorini. What property crime does exist tends to be from the less desirable tourists and criminals from the poorer states near to Greece. If you see the police on the island they will usually be drinking coffee or chatting to colleagues. But be warned, if you do transgress the rules, the police can be quite heavy handed.

The advice is of course be careful; however, I have accidentally left expensive items in public places in the past, only to return many hours later to find them just where I left them.

With regard to valuable items and money left in your hotel, again I have never heard of any problems. The room cleaning staff, I have met in the past, have proved totally honest and as long as you lock the windows and doors you should have no need to worry. Sadly there have been a few incidents of cars being broken into, especially when the owners leave valuables on show. So the rule is when you leave the car, put valuables in the boot and it is also worthwhile leaving the glove compartment open and empty.

In the event of a loss of a valuable item, remember that if you are insured, your insurance company will need written confirmation that the loss was reported to the local police.

The second category is safety with respect to the activities you participate in during your stay. Safety in Greece is less stringently policed than in the UK or US, so when you are out and about, and especially with children, extra care should be taken. To give an example, the walls around the caldera edge in Fira are low and on the other side there is a precipitous drop down into the sea, one slip could be fatal.

Being abroad you should also take extra care when driving. Although the Greeks are mostly good drivers, compared to say the Italians, there does seem to be an unofficial rule that many follow, to the effect that they should not purely concentrate on driving their vehicle. Mobile phones, eating and drinking and even doing paperwork should all be a part of the driving experience!

Keep in mind though that if *you* are not experienced at driving on

the right, mistakes can easily be made. It is a sobering sight on your travels, to see so many memorial boxes by the side of the road, especially by the cliff roads around the island. Sadly, in 2013 there were a number of fatal accidents on the island's cliff roads, primarily where crash barriers had not been installed, or did not cover an area where there was a steep drop.

As far as scooters, motorbikes and quad bikes are concerned, these are the most dangerous modes of transport on the island. You will see these being driven correctly with the riders mostly wearing crash helmets, but usually only with shorts and T-shirts being worn. Sadly I have seen the damage tarmac and gravel can do to human flesh even at slow speeds!

In Fira as in most towns, pavements are usually very narrow or non-existent, so extra care should be taken when walking in anywhere other than the pedestrianised areas.

One further point is not to trust the zebra crossings, in Greece these mean little although the rules do give the pedestrian "the right of way".

On the beach

If you have young children, just be a little careful on the beaches, as the currents can dredge out small holes in the seabed. This can be a shock to a child who finds that one minute they are in water a foot deep and the next up to their necks.

Swimming shoes

A recommended purchase is a pair of swimming shoes. They slip on and have a rubberised sole to protect you against hot sand, sharp rocks and sea urchins. They can be purchased at most beach-shops and large supermarkets and cost around 10€.

Hints and tips

Batteries

All the usual international battery sizes are available in the supermarkets at equivalent or cheaper prices than back home, but make sure you bring the battery chargers for your mobile phone, pda, etc.

Currency conversion

As the main currencies are unstable at the time of going to press, I have not included a currency rate in this edition. The latest exchange rates are available on our website, www.atoz-guides.com

Distance conversion

1 mile = 1.61 kilometres

Donkeys

Donkeys and mules in Santorini are part of the native charm of the island and can be loads of fun. During the summer the main business of the day is carting the tourists up and down the endless steep steps that connect Fira town to the small port below and to Ammoudi harbour. They are extremely adept at negotiating the steps, but they do have a tendency to go very fast and take the bends like the Road Runner.

Electricity

The electricity on Santorini and throughout Greece is 220V. You can purchase the two pin adaptors at the local electricity shops. So if you do not already own one, it may be cheaper to purchase them on the island.

Electric razors

Some accommodation on the island have dedicated 220V razor points in the bathrooms, but if not the adaptors sold on the island will take a twin pin razor plug.

Google Earth

For those with web access, an interesting and informative site is:-

www.earth.google.com

Here you can view satellite images of Santorini, but will need to download the free basic version software. Once downloaded, for quick access to satellite images of Santorini, add the following coordinates into the top left-hand corner box and press search. This will take you to Fira.

36 25 06.47N 25 25 55.19E

Google Street View

In the last few years, the Google map car has been collecting data and photographs across the Greece to add the country to those already covered by their 'Google Street Maps'. For Santorini, the main towns and tourist sites are now covered, To view 'Street Views', you need to enter 'Google Earth' and drag the orange man icon (*at the top right-hand side of the screen*) to the desired area.

Hair dryers

Many hotels and apartments supply a hairdryer in the room. If important, it is advisable to check with your tour-company or hotel before leaving home.

Internet connections

Most hotels offer WiFi facilities to guests with their own laptops, tablets or smartphones and larger hotels usually have an Internet room. In the main towns and resorts on the island many of the bars and cafés now also offer free WiFi to their customers. Alternatively, tourist resorts usually have at least one Internet Café, with the cost being around 3€ an hour, making it a cost effective way of contacting home and retrieving your emails. Remember though to take your important email addresses with you!

Laundry

If your hotel or apartments don't have a laundry service, there are quality laundry services in all the main resorts. So one solution to that bulging suitcase is to bring less and let the laundry take care of the problem.

Mobile phones

Many mobile phone companies now offer reduced cost call packages for when you are abroad, but you will have to contact them and enquire what offers are available at the time of your trip. Also remember to get your phone unblocked for international calls before you leave home.

Police

There are police stations in nearly every large village or town. You will recognize the police station by the Greek flag flying from the building and of course by the police vehicles parked outside.

On Santorini there is also a tourist police service (*Touristiki Astinomia*) for more holiday related problems. You will find the office of the tourist police in the same building as the island police in Fira.

The tourist police also supply information and brochures on the island and help in searching for accommodation.

Contact telephone numbers:

```
Fira Police     : 22860 22649
Oia Police      : 22860 71954
Tourist Police  : Dial 171
```

Post

As it is a tradition with us Brits to send home the usual "wish you were here" cards, I will cover posting on the island, but remember even if you post your cards soon after your arrival, it is highly likely you will be home before your cards!

The cost of the postcards and the stamps required for the UK/US is very low and you can purchase both in the supermarkets.

The Greek postal service is ELTA and post offices can be found in all the larger towns and are usually open from 07:30 to 14:00. Post boxes are coloured bright yellow and the post-office signs are yellow and blue.

Santorini National Airport

Sadly this information will only be of interest when you are returning home. The facilities are modern and as comfortable as any departure area. Once you pass through passport control, there are toilets, a café supplying drinks and snacks and a small duty-free shop selling the usual cigarettes, booze and a selection of those last-minute present ideas.

A shuttle bus service runs regularly throughout the season between the airport and Fira until 22:00 at night. Tel.: 22860 28400

Shoes

As I have mentioned elsewhere in the book, the vast majority of roads and alleyways on Santorini are cobbled with the local volcanic stone. It is therefore advisable to wear good walking shoes, or the soles of your feet may suffer from a day's walking on these uneven surfaces.

Spelling

On your travels and in printed material such as signs and menus, you will see names and places spelt in a variety of different ways. Do not be put off by the spelling, especially when you are trying to find somewhere, if it sounds the same, it probably is!

Sunbeds and parasols

If you are going to be a regular visit to the beach, rather than hire a parasol at an average of about 2.50€ a day, it may be cost-effective to buy one from one of the beachside supermarkets (*between 10 and 15€*). If you don't have a car and you are put off at the thought of carrying it back to your accommodation each day, you can ask nicely at the supermarket where you purchased it and they may allow you to leave it there overnight.

The same goes with the sunbeds; a good lilo can be purchased for around 10€ (*a sunbed is between 2 and 3€ a day*) and gives you the added advantage of being able to use it in the sea. Many supermarkets have a compressor that they may allow you to use, so you can deflate it at the end of the day and take it back to your accommodation, or as before, ask nicely at the supermarket and they may allow you to leave it there.

Telephoning

Many apartments and hotels now have phones in the room, although the cost of phoning home can be high. Alternatively many main landline providers in the UK and US as well as independent telephone prefix companies offer very low cost or even free international calls to Greece. It may therefore be cost effective to text relatives with your room telephone number and ask them to phone you. Remember Greece is 2 hours ahead of UK time and 7 hours ahead of US EDT.

Public telephones are to be found throughout the island, but remember, even in this age of mobile phones, there can be a queue of holidaymakers waiting to phone home, especially in resorts in the early evening.

To phone the UK the prefix is 0044 and you drop the first zero of the UK number, i.e. a London number that starts 020.....would translate into 0044 20.... To phone the US the code is 011 and then the full number required.

To phone Greece from outside the country, the prefix is 0030 and the area prefix for Santorini is 22860.

One further option for phoning home is to use Skype, although a number of the Internet Cafes have Skype loaded, it is best to bring a headset or Skype phone with you, as not all cafes supply them. If you are familiar with Skype, you will know that phone calls home will only cost cents, compared with euro with alternative services.

Tipping

Tipping is an awkward subject to cover as it is obviously dependent on the quality of service you have received and at your personal discretion. The service you receive on Santorini should be very good and if you take an average price for an evening meal for two of 60€, a tip of 10% is not excessive and quite acceptable. The local wages are low and it may also be courteous and prudent to tip within these limits.

Toilet paper

A delicate subject, but an important one. Due to the small bore of waste pipes that are used in Greece, it is a rule that toilet paper is not flushed, but deposited in the bin by the toilet. Although this can be a little embarrassing for some, it is better than having to call on the manager of your accommodation to help unblock the toilet. However, the bins are emptied on a regular basis and shouldn't cause a problem.

Water

Don't drink the tap water on Santorini. The Cyclades islands have a general problem with piped water supplies, the mineral content is very high, and since there has been no successful solution at the island's desalination plant, anything you drink should be bottled. For bathing and general washing feel free and safe to use tap water.

Water conservation is high priority and considered important on the island, since it is either expensively produced at the desalination plant or imported from the mainland and visitors should respect this. All kiosks sell bottled water, but more reasonable prices can be found at larger supermarkets.

For the very latest tips and information, please visit our website at:-

www.atoz-guides.com

Tony Oswin

Weddings, Honeymoons and Romance

Weddings

Santorini has become one of the most popular destinations for both weddings and honeymoons, especially as more and more couples are deciding to arrange to have their special day abroad. The spectacular and unique scenery, the fabulous weather, the breathtaking sunsets, the romantic atmosphere and the deep blue sea, attract couples from all over the world to take their vows and celebrate their new life with a honeymoon straight out of the picture books.

There are numerous companies offering to organise your wedding on Santorini, as a quick check on the internet will confirm. Whether you are planning a civil wedding, catholic wedding, orthodox wedding, or a vow renewal ceremony, there are companies that can coordinate the simplest to the most complex ceremony. Most offer either a total package, or will organise those parts that you prefer not to control yourselves. Whichever route you take, the following list contains the main issues:-

Booking the hotel for yourselves and your guests

Booking the church or venue

Organising the Greek marriage license and certificate

The translation and authentication of all documents

Hair and beauty services

Organising the reception, food and entertainment

Floral arrangements

Wedding cake

Photographer

Transportation needs

The notification of the wedding must be posted on the announcement board of the particular community at least 7 days before the service.

To give you an idea of the documents that you will have to supply (*at least one month in advance*) are:-

- Birth certificates of the bride and groom.

- An official document confirming that neither party is presently married. If one or both have been previously married, a divorce certificate(*s*) is required.

- Both the above must be in both English and Greek. The Greek consulate, in the couple's country of residence, must complete translations.

- Photocopies of the bride and grooms passports.

- Confirmation of the profession of the bride and groom.

- Full names of the parents of both the bride and groom.

- The religious denomination of both the bride and the groom.

Civil weddings can take place almost anywhere on Santorini. The most popular locations are in Fira, Firostefani and Imerovigli, all on the western side of Santorini, where the stunning scenery makes an ideal backdrop for a wedding. Some of the more unusual venues include a ceremony at a beautiful old mansion, at a traditional vineyard, or on a private veranda overlooking the caldera.

However, one thing to take into account whatever the style of wedding is that Santorini is a very popular location and can get booked up for a year or more in advance. It is never too early to start planning and to confirm whether your preferred wedding date is available.

Please keep in mind that not all the web sites you will find through the internet regarding wedding coordination in Santorini, are from legal wedding planners. My advice would be first to check on potential companies offering their service on the internet, but then to contact the tourist office on the island, or one of the quality hotels and check which they recommend.

Whether you want an intimate ceremony with just the two of you, a small circle of close family and friends, or dance the night away with a hundred guests, Santorini will delight and amaze all.

Anniversaries and special occasions

Would you love to re-live your special wedding day by taking your vows again? Or on the contrary, was your wedding day not the way you had always dreamt of, due to weather, anxiety, rush or limited budget? If so, then Santorini is just the place to organise that special occasion and I have no doubt the memories will last forever.

Glossary of Greek words and phrases

Below, I have included a few useful words with their Greek counterparts. Although the majority of Greeks on the island speak some level of English, with many being fluent, I have found that they really appreciate visitors attempting their language, even if you make a proverbial *pig's ear* of it!

Yes	Nay
No	Orhee
Good morning	Kalimaira
Good afternoon/evening	Kalispaira
Please	Parakalo
Thank you	Efkaristo
No, thank you	Okhee efkaristo
The bill please	To logargiasmo parakalo, or simply make a gesture in the air as though you were signing your name.....it works!
Hello/Goodbye (*singular/informal*)	Yiassou
Hello/Goodbye (*plural/formal*)	Yiassas
How much	Poso Kani
Coffee	Kafé
Tea	Chi
OK	Endaksi

Where is	Pooh eeneh
Do you speak English	Meelahteh ahnggleekah
I don't understand	Dhehn kahtahlahvehno
Can I have	Boro nah ehkho
Can we have	Boroomeh nah ehkhoomeh
I'd like	Thah eethehlah
Tomorrow	Avrio
Today	Seemaira
Toilets	To tooalettes
Wine	Krassi
Good	Kahloss
Bad	Kahkoss
Bank	Trapeeza
Police	Astinomeea
Doctor	Yatdros
Now	Tora
What is the time	Ti ora ine
Cheers	Yammas
Sorry/excuse me	Signomee

Greek timeline

Date	Event
2700 - 1450 B.C.	The period of the Minoan civilisation. The term Minoan was coined by Arthur Evans at the beginning of the 20th century. He was the archaeologist who excavated Knossos on Crete. He believed he had found the palace of the fabled King Minos...hence Minoan civilisation
1450 - 1100	The Mycenaeans are the dominant civilisation on mainland Greece and in the Aegean
1100 - 800	The Greek Dark Ages
776	First Olympic Games
circa 750	The start of early Greek culture. Homer creates the epics *The Iliad* and *The Odyssey*
508	Athens becomes a democratic state
490 & 480	Athenians defeat the Persians at the battles of Marathon (*490 B.C.*) and Salamis (*480 B.C.*)
472-410	Athens flourishes. Most of the famous Greek plays are written during this period
460-370	Hippocrates, the "father of medicine"
404	Sparta defeats Athens at the end of the Peloponnesian Wars (*431 - 404*)
338	King Philip of Macedonia takes control of Greece
336	Kind Philip is murdered, most likely by Alexander and his mother
336-323	Alexander the Great, son of King Philip, conquers most of the known world, as far as India
146	Rome conquers Greece and subjugates it as part of the Roman Empire

Early Roman timeline

Date	Event
509 B.C.	Traditional founding of the Roman Republic
396	Romans capture Estruscan city of Veii
390	Rome is sacked by Gauls after its army is slaughtered at the river Allia
275	The Pharos lighthouse at Alexandria is finished
264-241	First Punic War
218-201	Second Punic War
216	At Cannae, Rome suffers its worst defeat to the Carthaginian Hannibal
202	Hannibal is decisively defeated at Zama
200-196	Second Macedonian war
192-188	War with Antiochus III
171-167	Third Macedonian war
149-146	Third Punic War
146	City of Carthage is destroyed
133	Tiberius Gracchus introduces novel reforms including land grants to the poor and food distribution; he is murdered
123	Gaius Gracchus, brother of Tiberius is also murdered after initiating reforms along the same lines
107	Gaius Marius is elected consul; begins major reforms of army
88	Rome grants citizenship to all free adult males in Italy
82	Sulla becomes dictator

77	Senate chooses Pompey to put down Sertorius's rebellious army in Spain
73	Uprising of slaves led by Spartacus
71	Crassus and Pompey defeat Spartacus
60	Pompey, Crassus and Caesar form the First Triumvirate
59	Caesar elected consul
58-51	Gallic Wars conquest of Gaul by Julius Caesar
53	Crassus dies at the battle of Carrhae
49	Caesar defeats Pompey at Ilerda in Spain. Crosses Rubicon river; initiating civil war
48	At battle of Pharsalus Caesar defeats Pompey
46	Caesar becomes dictator
44	Brutus, Cassius and other senators assassinate Caesar
43	Octavian, Antony, and Lepidus form Second Triumvirate
42	Antony and Octavian defeat Brutus and Cassius at the battle of Philippi; destroying the last republican army
40	The Roman Senate makes Herod the Great King of Judea
33	Civil war between the armies of Octavian and Antony
31	Octavian crushes the naval forces of Antony and Cleopatra at the battle of Actium
27 B.C.	Octavian takes the title of Imperator Caesar Augustus; the empire begins

Tony Oswin

Imperial Rome timeline

Date	Event
27-14 A.D.	Reign of Augustus as Emperor
9 A.D.	Three Roman legions annihilated by Germanic tribes at the Battle of the Teutoburg Forest
14-37	Reign of Tiberius
37-41	Reign of Caligula
41	The mad emperor Caligula is stabbed to death
41-54	Reign of Claudius
43	Claudius orders the invasion of Britain
54-68	Reign of Nero
64	Great fire in Rome. Persecution of Christians
66	Beginning of Jewish revolt
69	The Year of The Four Emperors
69-79	Reign of Vespasian
70	The city of Jerusalem is virtually wiped out by Titus
79-81	Reign of Titus
79	Eruption of Mt. Vesuvius; the twin cities of Pompeii and Herculaneum are buried in ash
80	Colosseum (*Flavian Amphitheatre*) opens
81-96	Reign of Domitian
85	Agricola's campaigns in Britain end
98-117	Reign of Trajan
101-106	Trajan conquers Dacia. Arabia becomes a province

112-113	Trajan's Forum and Column dedicated
115-117	Jewish revolt
132-135	Bar Cochba's revolt; final Diaspora of the Jews. Hadrian's Villa built at Tivoli. Hadrian's Wall built in Britain
142	Wall of Antoninus Pius built north of Hadrian's Wall
165-167	Rome suffers from severe plague
162-178	Marcus Aurelius campaigns in Germanic Wars (*played by Richard Harris in the film Gladiator*)
180-192	The son of Marcus Aurelius, the egotistical Commodus is Emperor. In 192 his chief concubine has him murdered by strangulation
208-211	Severus campaigns in Britain. Arch of Septimius Severus erected
211 - 217	Caracalla is Roman Emperor
284-305	Diocletian's Reign
306-337	Constantine's Reign
312	The Emperor Constantine converts to Christianity. The Edict of Milan grants legal rights to Christians
325	The Council of Nicea – to agree the future of the Christian Church
330	Constantine declares Constantinople capital of a Christian Empire
circa 372	The Huns conquer the Ostrogoths
378	Battle of Adrianople, eastern Emperor Valens is killed by the Goths
379-395	Reign of Theodosius
395	Death of Theodosius I, final division into an Eastern and a Western Empire

396-398	The Visigoths ravage Greece
402	Ravenna becomes the capital of the western empire
410	Rome is sacked by the Visigoths
418	Visigoths settle in Aquitaine with capital at Toulouse
429	The Vandals cross from Spain to Africa
436	Last Roman troops leave Britain
441	The Huns defeat the Romans at Naissus
circa 450	Beginning of Anglo-Saxon settlements in Britain
451	Aetius defeats Attila at the Catalaunian Plain
453	Council of Chalcedon: Constantinople wins ecclesiastical supremacy over Alexandria
455	The Vandals sack Rome
476	Romulus Augustulus - last emperor of the west is forced from his throne by the Germanic chieftain Odoacer, who is proclaimed King of Italy
532-537	Justinian builds the Church of Hagia Sophia
533-534	Re-conquest of North Africa from the Vandals
535-555	Re-conquest of Italy from the Goths
541-543	Great Plague
548	Death of the Empress Theodora
568	The Lombards invade Italy
681	The First Bulgarian Empire is formed
690's	Muslims conquer Byzantine North Africa
717-718	Muslims lay siege to Constantinople
1453	Fall of Byzantine Empire when Turks capture Constantinople

Beaches and attractions

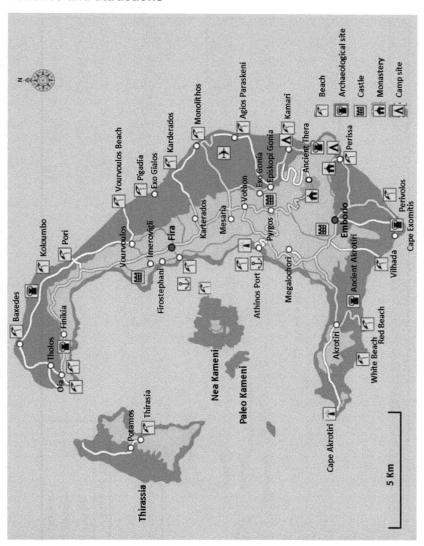

Map of Fira

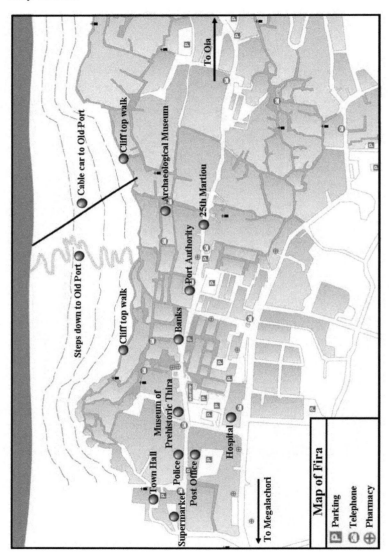

Map of the archaeological site of Akrotiri

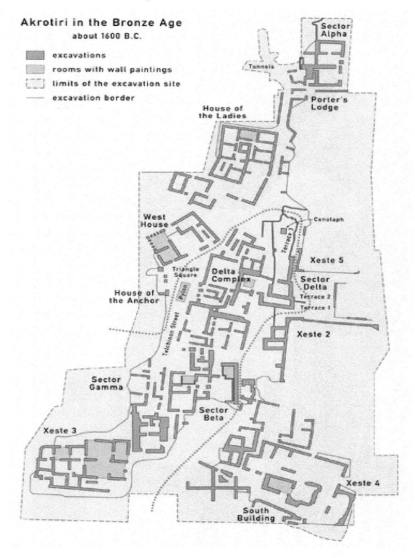

Akrotiri in the Bronze Age
about 1600 B.C.

excavations
rooms with wall paintings
limits of the excavation site
excavation border

Map of Ancient Thera

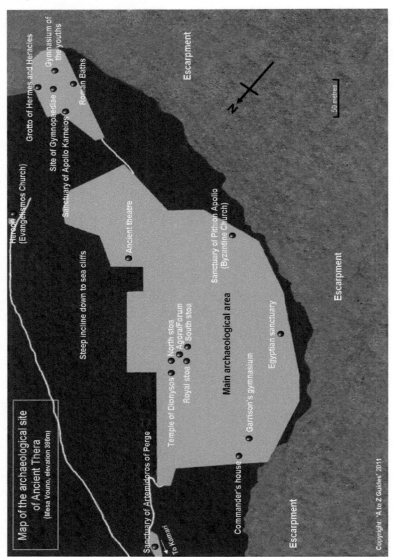

Acknowledgements and web sites of interest:

I would like to thank the following for their help in the writing of this book and the creation of the 'A to Z' website.

The people of Santorini
Athina Dimitropoulou, Amerisa Suites Hotel
Design & Digital Creative by www.verkko.co.uk
Walter I. Friedrich, Dept. of Earth Sciences, University of Aarhus

I have also included web pages that you may find of interest before your visit to the island.

www.greeka.com
www.paleologosco.com
www.amerisa.gr
www.santorini-hotels.info

For further information and the latest news from Santorini, visit our website:-

www.atoz-guides.com

Your 'A to Z Travel Club' password:-

Akrotiri

2018

JANUARY

Mo	Tu	We	Th	Fr	Sa	Su
1	2	3	4	5	6	7
8	9	10	11	12	13	14
15	16	17	18	19	20	21
22	23	24	25	26	27	28
29	30	31				

FEBRUARY

Mo	Tu	We	Th	Fr	Sa	Su
			1	2	3	4
5	6	7	8	9	10	11
12	13	14	15	16	17	18
19	20	21	22	23	24	25
26	27	28				

MARCH

Mo	Tu	We	Th	Fr	Sa	Su
			1	2	3	4
5	6	7	8	9	10	11
12	13	14	15	16	17	18
19	20	21	22	23	24	25
26	27	28	29	30	31	

APRIL

Mo	Tu	We	Th	Fr	Sa	Su
						1
2	3	4	5	6	7	8
9	10	11	12	13	14	15
16	17	18	19	20	21	22
23	24	25	26	27	28	29
30						

MAY

Mo	Tu	We	Th	Fr	Sa	Su
	1	2	3	4	5	6
7	8	9	10	11	12	13
14	15	16	17	18	19	20
21	22	23	24	25	26	27
28	29	30	31			

JUNE

Mo	Tu	We	Th	Fr	Sa	Su
				1	2	3
4	5	6	7	8	9	10
11	12	13	14	15	16	17
18	19	20	21	22	23	24
25	26	27	28	29	30	

JULY

Mo	Tu	We	Th	Fr	Sa	Su
						1
2	3	4	5	6	7	8
9	10	11	12	13	14	15
16	17	18	19	20	21	22
23	24	25	26	27	28	29
30	31					

AUGUST

Mo	Tu	We	Th	Fr	Sa	Su
		1	2	3	4	5
6	7	8	9	10	11	12
13	14	15	16	17	18	19
20	21	22	23	24	25	26
27	28	29	30	31		

SEPTEMBER

Mo	Tu	We	Th	Fr	Sa	Su
					1	2
3	4	5	6	7	8	9
10	11	12	13	14	15	16
17	18	19	20	21	22	23
24	25	26	27	28	29	30

OCTOBER

Mo	Tu	We	Th	Fr	Sa	S
1	2	3	4	5	6	7
8	9	10	11	12	13	14
15	16	17	18	19	20	21
22	23	24	25	26	27	28
29	30	31				

NOVEMBER

Mo	Tu	We	Th	Fr	Sa	Su
			1	2	3	4
5	6	7	8	9	10	11
12	13	14	15	16	17	18
19	20	21	22	23	24	25
26	27	28	29	30		

DECEMBER

Mo	Tu	We	Th	Fr	Sa	Su
					1	2
3	4	5	6	7	8	9
10	11	12	13	14	15	16
17	18	19	20	21	22	23
24	25	26	27	28	29	30
31						

Notepad

Notepad

Lightning Source UK Ltd.
Milton Keynes UK
UKHW02f1913070318
319079UK00008B/168/P